CONTENTS

Sales Tech Fundamentals	1
Introduction	3
Part 1: Foundational Concepts	7
Part 2: Building a Modern Sales Strategy	13
Part 3: Technology Integration in Sales	19
Part 4: Lead Generation and Qualification	26
Part 5: Effective Sales Engagement	35
Part 6: Optimizing Sales Processes	43
Part 7: Sales Automation and AI	56
Part 8: Sales and Marketing Alignment	70
Part 9: Case Studies and Real-Life Applications	89
Part 10: Advanced Sales Strategies	103
Part 11: Managing and Scaling Sales Teams	118
Part 12: Future Trends in Sales	133
Part 13: Tools and Resources	148
Conclusion and Key Takeaways	156

SALES TECH FUNDAMENTALS

The Sales Professional's Guide to
AI, Automation & Analytics

Kim Domingo Reyes

No part of this book may be reproduced or transmitted in any form whatsoever, electronic, or mechanical, including photocopying, recording, or by any informational storage or retrieval system without express permission from the author or publisher.

Copyright © 2024 RJK Publishing

All rights reserved

INTRODUCTION

The Evolution of Sales in the Digital Era

The world of sales has undergone a dramatic transformation in recent years, driven by the rapid advancement of technology. Gone are the days when sales professionals relied solely on cold calls, face-to-face meetings, and gut instincts to close deals. Today, the most successful sales teams leverage a powerful combination of human skills and cutting-edge technology to achieve unprecedented results.

In the digital era, customers are more informed, connected, and empowered than ever before. They have access to a wealth of information at their fingertips and can easily compare products, services, and prices across multiple vendors. As a result, traditional sales techniques that once worked well are now less effective, and sales professionals must adapt to stay relevant and competitive.

Understanding Tech-Powered Sales

Tech-powered sales is a new paradigm that embraces the integration of advanced technologies into the sales process. It involves leveraging tools such as artificial intelligence (AI), machine learning, automation, and data analytics to enhance the efficiency, productivity, and effectiveness of sales teams.

By harnessing the power of technology, sales professionals can gain deeper insights into customer behavior, preferences, and needs. They can automate repetitive tasks, freeing up more time for high-value activities such as building relationships and closing deals. Additionally, tech-powered sales enables organizations to scale their efforts, reach a wider audience, and deliver personalized experiences to each and every prospect.

Key Objectives of This Book

This book aims to provide sales professionals, managers, and leaders with a comprehensive guide to succeeding in the era of tech-powered sales. Through practical insights, real-world examples, and actionable strategies, readers will learn how to:

- Understand the impact of technology on modern sales and adapt to the changing landscape
- Develop a tech-powered sales strategy that aligns with their organization's goals and customer needs
- Build and optimize a sales tech stack that includes essential tools for automation, analytics, and engagement
- Leverage AI and machine learning to improve lead generation, qualification, and conversion rates
- Implement effective multi-channel communication strategies for personalized outreach and engagement
- Streamline sales processes, improve productivity, and make data-driven decisions
- Foster alignment between sales and marketing teams to create a unified revenue strategy
- Prepare for the future of sales by staying up-to-date with emerging trends and technologies

Whether you are a seasoned sales veteran looking to update your skills or a new professional seeking to start your career on the right foot, this book will provide you with the knowledge and tools you need to thrive in the tech-powered sales era.

So, let's dive in and explore the exciting world of tech-powered sales together!

Tech-Powered Sales: Achieve Superhuman Sales Skills

The Evolution of Sales in the Digital Era

The world of sales has undergone a dramatic transformation in recent years, driven by the rapid advancement of technology. Gone are the days when sales professionals relied solely on cold calls, face-to-face meetings, and gut instincts to close deals. Today, the most successful sales teams leverage a powerful combination of human skills and cutting-edge technology to achieve unprecedented results.

In the digital era, customers are more informed, connected, and empowered than ever before. They have access to a wealth of information at their fingertips and can easily compare products, services, and prices across multiple vendors. As a result, traditional sales techniques that once worked well are now less effective, and sales professionals must adapt to stay relevant and competitive.

Understanding Tech-Powered Sales

Tech-powered sales is a new paradigm that embraces the integration of advanced technologies into the sales process. It involves leveraging tools such as artificial intelligence (AI), machine learning, automation, and data analytics to enhance the efficiency, productivity, and effectiveness of sales teams.

By harnessing the power of technology, sales professionals can gain deeper insights into customer behavior, preferences, and needs. They can automate repetitive tasks, freeing up more time for high-value activities such as building relationships and closing deals. Additionally, tech-powered sales enables organizations to scale their efforts, reach a wider audience, and deliver personalized experiences to each and every prospect.

Key Objectives of This Book

This book aims to provide sales professionals, managers, and leaders with a comprehensive guide to succeeding in the era of tech-powered sales. Through practical insights, real-world examples, and actionable strategies, readers will learn how to:

- Understand the impact of technology on modern sales and adapt to the changing landscape
- Develop a tech-powered sales strategy that aligns with their organization's goals and customer needs
- Build and optimize a sales tech stack that includes essential tools for automation, analytics, and engagement
- Leverage AI and machine learning to improve lead generation, qualification, and conversion rates
- Implement effective multi-channel communication strategies for personalized outreach and engagement
- Streamline sales processes, improve productivity, and make data-driven decisions
- Foster alignment between sales and marketing teams to create a unified revenue strategy
- Prepare for the future of sales by staying up-to-date with emerging trends and technologies

Whether you are a seasoned sales veteran looking to update your skills or a new professional seeking to start your career on the right foot, this book will provide you with the knowledge and tools you need to thrive in the tech-powered sales era.

So, let's dive in and explore the exciting world of tech-powered sales together!

PART 1: FOUNDATIONAL CONCEPTS

The Impact of Technology on Sales

The sales landscape has evolved dramatically in recent years, largely due to the rapid advancement and widespread adoption of technology. From the way salespeople prospect and engage with leads to how they close deals and manage customer relationships, technology has reshaped nearly every aspect of the sales process.

One of the most significant impacts of technology on sales is the shift in customer behavior and expectations. In today's digital age, buyers are more informed and empowered than ever before. They can easily access a wealth of information about products, services, and companies through online search engines, social media, and review sites. As a result, they often enter the sales process with a clearer understanding of their needs and options, and they expect salespeople to provide personalized, relevant, and value-added insights.

Technology has also transformed the way salespeople work and collaborate. With the proliferation of cloud-based platforms, mobile devices, and productivity tools, sales teams can now access critical data and resources from anywhere, at any time. This has enabled greater flexibility, agility, and efficiency in sales operations, allowing teams to respond quickly to market changes and customer demands.

Moreover, technology has introduced new channels and touchpoints for sales engagement. From social selling on LinkedIn to chatbots and virtual assistants, salespeople now have a wide array of tools at their disposal to connect with prospects and customers in more targeted, interactive, and scalable ways. These digital channels have expanded the reach and impact of sales efforts, enabling organizations to tap into new markets and customer segments.

However, the impact of technology on sales is not without its challenges. As sales tech stacks become increasingly complex and data-driven, salespeople must develop new skills and adapt to new ways of working. They must learn how to effectively leverage technology to enhance their productivity and performance, while also maintaining the human touch and emotional intelligence that are critical for building trust and rapport with buyers.

Essential Sales Skills in the Modern Era

While technology has transformed many aspects of sales, it has not diminished the importance of fundamental sales skills. In fact, in the modern era of tech-powered sales, certain skills have become even more critical for success. Here are some of the essential sales skills that professionals must master to thrive in today's competitive landscape:

Adaptability: With the rapid pace of technological change and market disruption, salespeople must be able to quickly adapt to new tools, processes, and customer expectations. They need to be comfortable with ambiguity and able to pivot their strategies and tactics based on real-time data and feedback.

Curiosity: In a world of information overload, salespeople must have a insatiable curiosity to continuously learn and stay up-to-date with industry trends, customer needs, and competitive landscapes. They should be proactive in seeking out new insights and perspectives that can help them better serve their clients and differentiate their offerings.

Empathy: Despite the rise of automation and AI, sales is still fundamentally a human-to-human interaction. Salespeople must be able to put themselves in their customers' shoes, understand their challenges and aspirations, and communicate with genuine care and concern. Empathy is key to building trust, credibility, and long-term partnerships.

Storytelling: In a noisy and crowded marketplace, salespeople must be able to cut through the clutter and capture the attention and imagination of their prospects. Storytelling is a powerful tool for creating emotional connections, communicating value, and inspiring action. Salespeople who can craft compelling narratives that resonate with their audience will be more effective in driving engagement and conversions.

Problem-solving: Ultimately, customers don't buy products or services; they buy solutions to their problems. Salespeople who can identify and diagnose customer pain points, and then prescribe tailored solutions that deliver measurable results, will be well-positioned for success. This requires a combination of analytical thinking, creativity, and resourcefulness.

Resilience: Sales can be a challenging and often unpredictable profession, with frequent rejections, setbacks, and failures. Salespeople must have the mental toughness and emotional resilience to bounce back from adversity, learn from their mistakes, and maintain a positive and proactive mindset. This requires a growth-oriented attitude and a commitment to continuous self-improvement.

Collaboration: In today's complex and interconnected business environment, sales is rarely a solo endeavor. Salespeople must be able to work effectively across functions and departments, including marketing, customer success, product development, and finance. They need to be team players who can build consensus, share insights, and coordinate efforts to deliver a seamless customer experience.

By mastering these essential sales skills, professionals can leverage technology more effectively and create more value for their customers and their organizations. They can combine the efficiency and scalability of digital tools with the empathy and expertise of human interaction to achieve superhuman sales performance.

Combining Human Skills with Technological Tools

To succeed in the era of tech-powered sales, professionals must learn how to seamlessly blend their human skills with technological tools. This requires a mindset shift from seeing technology as a replacement for human interaction to viewing it as an enabler and enhancer of human potential.

One of the key ways to combine human skills with technology is through the use of data and analytics. By leveraging tools like customer relationship management (CRM) systems, marketing automation platforms, and business intelligence dashboards, salespeople can gain real-time insights into customer behavior, preferences, and buying patterns. They can use this data to personalize their outreach, tailor their messaging, and anticipate customer needs and objections.

However, data alone is not enough. Salespeople must also apply their human judgment, intuition, and creativity to turn data into actionable insights and strategies. They need to be able to interpret the numbers, identify patterns and anomalies, and extract meaningful stories and recommendations that resonate with customers on an emotional level.

Another way to blend human skills with technology is through the use of social selling techniques. By leveraging social media platforms like LinkedIn, Twitter, and Facebook, salespeople can build their personal brand, establish thought leadership, and engage with prospects and customers in more authentic and personalized ways. They can share relevant content, participate in industry conversations, and provide value-added insights that demonstrate their expertise and build trust.

Effective social selling involves a nuanced blend of automation and personalization. Sales professionals must avoid over-relying on generic templates or impersonal automated messages that may appear spammy. Instead, they should invest time in researching their potential customers, crafting customized outreach, and fostering genuine dialogue and relationship-building. This approach enhances the chances of connecting with prospects, establishing trust, and ultimately driving sales success.

Finally, salespeople can combine human skills with technology through the use of video and virtual communication tools. With the rise of remote work and digital selling, video has become an increasingly important channel for building rapport, demonstrating products, and closing deals. Salespeople who can master the art of virtual presence, using techniques like eye contact, active listening, and storytelling, can create more engaging and impactful sales experiences.

However, virtual selling also requires a different set of skills and mindsets than in-person selling. Salespeople must be able to adapt to technical challenges, manage distractions, and create a professional and polished environment, even from their home office. They need to be able to read digital body language, build trust through the screen, and create a sense of intimacy and connection without physical proximity.

Ultimately, the key to combining human skills with technological tools is to focus on the customer experience. Salespeople must use technology to enhance rather than replace human interaction, to create more value rather than just more noise, and to build relationships rather than just transactions. By striking the right balance between automation and personalization, efficiency and empathy, salespeople can achieve superhuman results and create lasting customer loyalty.

PART 2: BUILDING A MODERN SALES STRATEGY

Identifying Ideal Customer Profiles (ICPs)

One of the foundations of a successful tech-powered sales strategy is a deep understanding of your ideal customer profile (ICP). An ICP is a detailed description of the type of company that would benefit most from your product or service, and that represents the highest potential for long-term revenue and growth.

Defining your ICP involves a combination of quantitative and qualitative analysis, drawing on data from your CRM, marketing automation, and customer success platforms, as well as insights from your sales and customer-facing teams. Some key factors to consider when developing your ICP include:

Firmographics: What are the common characteristics of your best customers in terms of industry, company size, location, and revenue?

Technographics: What technologies do your ideal customers use, and how do they align with your product or service?

Business challenges: What are the specific pain points, goals, and priorities that your solution addresses for your ideal customers?

Buying behavior: How do your ideal customers typically make purchasing decisions, and who are the key stakeholders involved?

Success potential: Which customers have the highest likelihood of achieving success with your offering, based on factors like resources, maturity, and alignment?

By clearly defining your ICP, you can focus your sales and marketing efforts on the accounts that are most likely to convert, retain, and expand over time. You can develop targeted messaging, content, and campaigns that speak directly to the needs and interests of your ideal customers, and you can prioritize your outreach and engagement based on account fit and potential.

However, identifying your ICP is not a one-time exercise. As your business evolves and your market landscape changes, you need to continually refine and update your ICP based on new data and insights. You may need to segment your ICP into different tiers or sub-profiles based on specific criteria, or you may need to expand your ICP to include new industries or geographies.

To operationalize your ICP, you need to integrate it into your sales and marketing technology stack. This means using tools like lead scoring, account-based marketing, and predictive analytics to identify and prioritize accounts that match your ICP criteria. It also means training your sales team on how to recognize and engage with ICP accounts, and how to tailor their outreach and messaging accordingly.

By making your ICP a core part of your sales strategy and process, you can improve your efficiency, effectiveness, and alignment across the customer lifecycle. You can reduce waste and churn by focusing on the right accounts, and you can increase revenue and loyalty by delivering more personalized and valuable experiences to your ideal customers.

Developing a Value Narrative

Once you have identified your ideal customer profile, the next step is to develop a compelling value narrative that articulates the unique benefits and outcomes that your solution delivers for those customers. A value narrative is not just a list of features or capabilities; rather, it is a story that connects your offering to the specific challenges, goals, and aspirations of your target audience.

To craft an effective value narrative, you need to start by deeply understanding your customers' world. This means conducting research, interviews, and analysis to uncover the key trends, issues, and opportunities that are shaping their business and industry. It also means mapping out the different stakeholders and decision-makers involved in the buying process, and identifying their individual needs, preferences, and concerns.

Armed with this customer insight, you can then develop a value proposition that clearly articulates the tangible and measurable impact that your solution can have on your customers' business. This includes quantifying the potential return on investment, cost savings, revenue growth, or other metrics that matter most to your buyers. It also includes highlighting the unique differentiators and advantages that set your solution apart from competitors.

However, a value narrative is more than just a rational argument; it is also an emotional story that taps into the deeper desires and motivations of your customers. This means using customer success stories, case studies, and testimonials to bring your value proposition to life, and to show how your solution has transformed the lives and businesses of similar companies. It also means using visuals, metaphors, and other storytelling techniques to make your message more memorable and impactful.

To deliver your value narrative effectively, you need to equip your sales team with the right tools, content, and training. This includes developing sales playbooks, battle cards, and other resources that provide guidance on how to position your solution in different scenarios and conversations. It also includes creating a central repository of customer-facing content, such as presentations, demos, and proposals, that can be easily customized and repurposed for different accounts and opportunities.

Finally, to ensure that your value narrative resonates with customers and drives action, you need to continuously test, measure, and optimize its performance. This means tracking metrics like email open rates, content engagement, and conversion rates, and using that data to refine your messaging and tactics over time. It also means soliciting feedback from customers and prospects on what aspects of your value narrative are most compelling or confusing, and using that input to improve your overall sales and marketing strategy.

By developing a strong value narrative that is grounded in customer insight, backed by tangible proof points, and delivered with consistency and impact, you can differentiate your solution in a crowded market, shorten your sales cycles, and win more deals at higher margins. You can also build deeper and more lasting relationships with your customers by demonstrating your commitment to their success and your alignment with their goals.

Aligning Sales and Marketing

One of the biggest challenges in modern sales is the disconnect between sales and marketing teams. Too often, these functions operate in silos, with different goals, metrics, and processes that can lead to friction, inefficiency, and missed opportunities. To succeed in the era of tech-powered sales, it is essential to align sales and marketing around a common strategy, language, and customer experience.

The first step in aligning sales and marketing is to establish a shared understanding of your ideal customer profile and value narrative. This means involving both teams in the process of developing these foundational elements, and ensuring that they are reflected consistently across all touchpoints and channels. It also means creating a common set of metrics and KPIs that both teams can use to track progress and measure success.

One effective way to align sales and marketing is through the use of account-based marketing (ABM) strategies. ABM is a targeted approach that focuses on engaging and converting a specific set of high-value accounts that match your ICP. By aligning sales and marketing around a common set of target accounts, you can create a more personalized and integrated customer experience that spans the entire funnel, from awareness to advocacy.

To implement an ABM strategy, sales and marketing need to work together to identify and prioritize target accounts, develop custom content and campaigns for each account, and coordinate outreach and follow-up across channels. This requires a high degree of collaboration and communication between teams, as well as the use of specialized tools and platforms that can enable account-level tracking, messaging, and reporting.

Another way to align sales and marketing is through the use of sales enablement techniques. Sales enablement refers to the processes, content, and tools that help sales teams have more effective and productive conversations with prospects and customers. This includes things like product training, competitive intelligence, objection handling, and customer case studies.

By providing sales teams with the right enablement resources, marketing can help them to better understand an d articulate the value proposition, differentiate from competitors, and build trust and credibility with buyers. At the same time, by gathering feedback and insights from sales conversations, marketing can refine and optimize their content and campaigns to better address customer needs and concerns.

To truly achieve sales and marketing alignment, it is important to foster a culture of collaboration, experimentation, and continuous improvement. This means breaking down silos and encouraging cross-functional communication and feedback. It also means embracing a data-driven approach to decision-making, where both teams use shared metrics and insights to inform their strategies and tactics.

Some best practices for aligning sales and marketing include:

Establishing a lead handoff process: Clearly define when and how leads are passed from marketing to sales, and what criteria and actions are required for each stage of the funnel.

Conducting regular check-ins: Schedule weekly or bi-weekly meetings between sales and marketing leaders to review progress, share insights, and identify areas for improvement.

Creating a content calendar: Develop a shared calendar that maps out the key themes, topics, and assets that will be developed and promoted each quarter, aligned with sales priorities and customer needs.

Implementing closed-loop reporting: Use marketing automation and CRM tools to track the full customer journey from initial touch to closed deal, and use that data to optimize campaigns and content over time.

By aligning sales and marketing around a shared vision and strategy, organizations can improve their efficiency, agility, and customer-centricity. They can create a more seamless and personalized experience for buyers, from initial awareness to post-sale support. And they can ultimately drive more revenue, loyalty, and growth in the long run.

PART 3: TECHNOLOGY INTEGRATION IN SALES

Understanding the Sales Tech Stack

To fully leverage the power of technology in sales, it is essential to understand the different components of the sales tech stack and how they work together to support the end-to-end sales process. A sales tech stack refers to the collection of tools, platforms, and systems that sales teams use to automate, streamline, and optimize their activities and workflows.

While the specific components of a sales tech stack can vary depending on the size, industry, and maturity of an organization, there are some common categories and examples that are widely used in modern sales. These include:

Customer Relationship Management (CRM): CRM platforms like Salesforce, HubSpot, and Microsoft Dynamics are the backbone of most sales tech stacks. They provide a centralized database for managing customer data, tracking interactions and activities, and forecasting pipeline and revenue.

Sales Engagement: Sales engagement tools like Outreach, SalesLoft, and Groove help sales reps to automate and personalize their outreach and follow-up across channels like email, phone, and social media. They can also provide analytics and insights on the effectiveness of different messaging and tactics.

Sales Intelligence: Sales intelligence platforms like ZoomInfo, DiscoverOrg, and Clearbit provide data and insights on prospects and accounts, including contact information, firmographics, technographics, and intent signals. They can help sales teams to identify and prioritize high-value targets and tailor their outreach accordingly.

Sales Enablement: Sales enablement tools like Highspot, Seismic, and Showpad help sales teams to access and deliver the right content and resources at the right time, based on the specific needs and stage of each deal. They can also provide analytics and feedback on content performance and engagement.

Sales Forecasting and Analytics: Sales forecasting and analytics tools like InsightSquared, Clari, and Aviso use machine learning and predictive modeling to provide real-time visibility and insights on pipeline health, deal risk, and revenue potential. They can help sales leaders to make data-driven decisions and adjustments to their strategies and tactics.

Conversational Intelligence: Conversational intelligence tools like Gong, Chorus, and ExecVision use natural language processing (NLP) and machine learning to analyze sales conversations and provide insights on topics, sentiment, and outcomes. They can help sales reps to improve their skills and performance, and to identify best practices and coaching opportunities.

To effectively integrate these different tools and platforms into a cohesive sales tech stack, organizations need to consider several key factors, such as:

Compatibility and integration: Ensuring that different tools can seamlessly share data and insights across the stack, without manual effort or duplication.

User adoption and enablement: Providing training, support, and incentives for sales reps to fully leverage the capabilities of each tool, and to incorporate them into their daily workflows and habits.

Data quality and governance: Establishing clear processes and standards for data entry, validation, and maintenance, to ensure the accuracy and reliability of insights and decisions.

Scalability and flexibility: Choosing tools that can adapt and grow with the changing needs and priorities of the sales organization, without requiring significant rework or replacement.

By carefully designing and optimizing their sales tech stack, organizations can unlock significant benefits in terms of efficiency, productivity, and performance. They can automate repetitive and low-value tasks, freeing up sales reps to focus on high-impact activities like building relationships and closing deals. They can also gain deeper and more actionable insights on customer needs, behaviors, and trends, enabling them to deliver more personalized and relevant experiences at scale.

Essential Tools for Sales Automation

Among the different components of the sales tech stack, automation tools are perhaps the most critical for modern sales teams. By automating repetitive and time-consuming tasks, sales reps can focus on more strategic and valuable activities, such as building relationships, solving complex problems, and closing deals.

Here are some of the essential tools for sales automation, along with their key features and benefits:

Email Automation: Email automation tools like Mailchimp, Constant Contact, and Pardot allow sales reps to create, schedule, and send personalized email campaigns at scale. They can also provide analytics and insights on email performance, such as open rates, click-through rates, and conversions.

CRM Automation: CRM automation tools like Salesforce Einstein, HubSpot Workflows, and Zoho CRM help sales reps to automate tasks like lead assignment, opportunity creation, and data entry. They can also provide predictive insights and recommendations on next best actions, based on historical data and machine learning algorithms.

Sales Cadence Automation: Sales cadence automation tools like Outreach, SalesLoft, and Yesware enable sales reps to create and execute multi-touch, multi-channel outreach sequences that span email, phone, social, and video. They can also provide real-time analytics and feedback on the effectiveness of different messaging and tactics.

Meeting Scheduling Automation: Meeting scheduling tools like Calendly, Chili Piper, and HubSpot Meetings allow sales reps to automate the process of booking and confirming meetings with prospects and customers. They can also sync with CRM and calendar systems to avoid double-booking and ensure seamless coordination.

Proposal and Contract Automation: Proposal and contract automation tools like PandaDoc, Conga Composer, and Qwilr help sales reps to create, send, and track professional-looking proposals and contracts. They can also integrate with CRM and e-signature platforms to streamline the approval and signing process.

Sales Reporting Automation: Sales reporting automation tools like Domo, Tableau, and Looker enable sales leaders to create and distribute customized dashboards and reports on key metrics and KPIs. They can also automate data extraction, transformation, and loading (ETL) processes to ensure data accuracy and timeliness.

To effectively leverage these automation tools, sales teams need to follow some best practices, such as:

Defining clear goals and metrics: Identifying the specific outcomes and indicators that each automation tool is intended to support, and tracking progress and impact over time.

Developing standardized processes: Establishing consistent and repeatable workflows and templates for each automation use case, and ensuring alignment and adoption across the sales team.

Providing adequate training and support: Equipping sales reps with the skills and knowledge needed to effectively use each automation tool, and providing ongoing coaching and feedback to optimize performance.

Monitoring and adjusting automation rules: Regularly reviewing and updating automation rules and settings based on changing business needs, customer preferences, and market conditions.

By strategically deploying and managing sales automation tools, organizations can achieve significant gains in terms of speed, accuracy, and scalability. They can reduce manual effort and errors, improve response times and relevance, and ultimately drive more revenue and growth.

Leveraging AI and Machine Learning for Sales

Artificial intelligence (AI) and machine learning (ML) are rapidly transforming the sales landscape, enabling organizations to process vast amounts of data, generate predictive insights, and automate complex decision-making processes. By leveraging AI and ML technologies, sales teams can gain a competitive edge in terms of efficiency, effectiveness, and customer experience.

Here are some of the key applications and benefits of AI and ML in sales:

Lead Scoring and Prioritization: AI-powered lead scoring models can analyze a wide range of data points, such as demographic, behavioral, and firmographic attributes, to predict the likelihood of a lead converting into a customer. This can help sales teams to prioritize their outreach and focus on the most promising opportunities.

Predictive Forecasting: ML algorithms can analyze historical sales data, market trends, and economic indicators to generate accurate and timely forecasts of future revenue and pipeline. This can help sales leaders to make data-driven decisions around resource allocation, territory planning, and quota setting.

Personalized Recommendations: AI-based recommendation engines can analyze customer data, such as purchase history, browsing behavior, and social media activity, to generate personalized product or service recommendations. This can help sales reps to cross-sell and upsell more effectively, and to deliver more relevant and valuable customer experiences.

Sentiment Analysis: Natural Language Processing (NLP) techniques can analyze the sentiment and emotion behind customer interactions, such as email exchanges, phone conversations, and social media posts. This can help sales reps to gauge customer satisfaction, identify potential issues or objections, and adapt their communication style accordingly.

Conversational AI: Chatbots and virtual assistants powered by AI can handle routine customer inquiries, qualify leads, and even schedule meetings and demos. This can help sales teams to scale their outreach and engagement efforts, while freeing up time for more complex and strategic interactions.

To successfully implement AI and ML in sales, organizations need to consider several key factors, such as:

Data Quality and Quantity: AI and ML models require large and diverse datasets to train and improve their performance over time. Organizations need to invest in data collection, cleansing, and enrichment processes to ensure the accuracy and completeness of their data.

Ethical and Transparent Use: AI and ML can raise concerns around privacy, bias, and fairness, particularly when used to make decisions that impact customers or employees. Organizations need to develop clear policies and guidelines around the ethical and transparent use of AI, and to provide adequate disclosure and consent mechanisms.

Human-Machine Collaboration: AI and ML should be viewed as a complement to, rather than a replacement for, human judgment and expertise. Sales teams need to develop a collaborative and symbiotic relationship with AI, leveraging its insights and recommendations while applying their own context and intuition.

Continuous Learning and Improvement: AI and ML models need to be continuously trained and updated based on new data and feedback, in order to maintain their accuracy and relevance over time. Organizations need to establish processes and metrics for monitoring and optimizing the performance of their AI and ML systems.

By strategically leveraging AI and ML technologies, sales organizations can unlock new levels of efficiency, agility, and customer-centricity. They can automate routine tasks, generate real-time insights, and deliver hyper-personalized experiences at scale. Ultimately, they can drive more revenue, loyalty, and competitive advantage in the era of intelligent, data-driven selling.

PART 4: LEAD GENERATION AND QUALIFICATION

Top of Funnel (TOFU) Strategies

The top of the funnel (TOFU) refers to the initial stages of the customer journey, where potential buyers first become aware of a problem or need, and start researching potential solutions. At this stage, the goal of sales and marketing is to attract and engage a wide audience of relevant prospects, and to start building trust and credibility with them.

Here are some effective TOFU strategies for tech-powered sales teams:

Content Marketing: Creating and distributing valuable, relevant, and consistent content that addresses the needs and interests of your target audience. This can include blog posts, whitepapers, eBooks, infographics, videos, and more. By providing educational and informative content, you can establish your brand as a thought leader and trusted resource in your industry.

Search Engine Optimization (SEO): Optimizing your website and content for relevant keywords and phrases that your target audience is searching for. This can help your brand to rank higher in search engine results pages (SERPs), and to attract more organic traffic to your site. By using tools like Google

Analytics and SEMrush, you can track your search performance and identify opportunities for improvement.

Social Media Marketing: Building and engaging a community of followers on social media platforms like LinkedIn, Twitter, Facebook, and Instagram. This can help you to expand your reach, share your content, and interact directly with your target audience. By using social listening and analytics tools, you can monitor conversations and sentiment around your brand and industry, and adapt your messaging and tactics accordingly.

Paid Advertising: Running targeted advertising campaigns on search engines, social media, and other digital channels to reach and engage your ideal customer profile. This can include pay-per-click (PPC) ads, display ads, sponsored content, and more. By using data and AI-powered targeting and optimization tools, you can improve the relevance and effectiveness of your ads, and maximize your return on ad spend (ROAS).

Influencer Marketing: Partnering with influential individuals or organizations in your industry to co-create and promote content, products, or events. This can help you to tap into the influencer's audience and credibility, and to generate more buzz and interest around your brand. By using influencer marketing platforms and tools, you can identify and recruit relevant influencers, and track the impact and ROI of your campaigns.

Event Marketing: Hosting or sponsoring events, webinars, or conferences that bring together your target audience around a common theme or topic. This can help you to generate leads, showcase your expertise, and build relationships with potential buyers. By using event management and marketing tools, you can streamline the planning and promotion of your events, and capture attendee data for follow-up and nurturing.

To optimize your TOFU strategies, it's important to align them with your overall sales and marketing goals, and to measure and analyze their performance regularly. Some key metrics to track include website traffic, content engagement, social media followers and interactions, ad clicks and conversions, and event registrations and attendees.

By using data and technology to inform and optimize your TOFU strategies, you can generate a steady stream of high-quality leads, and set the stage for successful lead nurturing and conversion down the funnel.

Middle of Funnel (MOFU) Tactics

The middle of the funnel (MOFU) refers to the stage of the customer journey where leads have expressed interest in your product or service, and are actively considering their options. At this stage, the goal of sales and marketing is to educate and engage leads, build trust and credibility, and move them closer to a purchase decision.

Here are some effective MOFU tactics for tech-powered sales teams:

Lead Nurturing: Developing and executing targeted email campaigns and sequences that provide relevant and valuable content to leads based on their interests, behaviors, and stage in the funnel. This can include educational content, case studies, product demos, and more. By using marketing automation and personalization tools, you can scale your lead nurturing efforts and deliver a more tailored and engaging experience to each lead.

Sales Enablement: Providing sales reps with the content, tools, and training they need to effectively engage and convert leads. This can include battle cards, objection handling guides, product collateral, and more. By using sales enablement platforms and analytics, you can ensure that reps have access to the most up-to-date and effective resources, and can track their usage and impact on sales performance.

Lead Scoring: Assigning scores or grades to leads based on their demographic, firmographic, and behavioral attributes, to prioritize and route them to the most appropriate sales rep or team. This can help you to focus your efforts on the most promising and sales-ready leads, and to avoid wasting time and resources on lower-quality or unqualified leads. By using lead scoring tools and models, you can automate and optimize your lead qualification process, and improve your conversion rates and sales velocity.

Account-Based Marketing (ABM): Targeting and engaging specific accounts or companies that fit your ideal customer profile, with personalized and coordinated campaigns across multiple channels and touchpoints. This can include targeted advertising, direct mail, personalized email and video, and more. By using ABM platforms and data, you can align your sales and marketing efforts around high-value accounts, and create a more consistent and compelling experience for key decision-makers and influencers.

Social Selling: Using social media platforms like LinkedIn and Twitter to research, connect with, and engage potential buyers and influencers. This can include sharing relevant content, commenting on posts, sending personalized messages, and more. By using social selling tools and techniques, sales reps can build their personal brand and network, establish trust and credibility with leads, and gather valuable insights and intelligence about their needs and challenges.

Webinars and Demos: Hosting live or on-demand webinars and product demonstrations that showcase your solution and its value to potential buyers. This can help you to educate and engage leads, answer their questions and objections, and move them closer to a purchase decision. By using webinar and demo platforms and analytics, you can streamline the planning and execution of your events, capture lead data and feedback, and measure their impact on pipeline and revenue.

To maximize the effectiveness of your MOFU tactics, it's

important to align them with your buyer personas and journey maps, and to continuously test and optimize them based on data and feedback. Some key metrics to track include email open and click-through rates, content engagement and sharing, lead scores and conversion rates, account engagement and penetration, and webinar and demo attendance and feedback.

By using technology and data to power your MOFU tactics, you can create a more personalized and valuable experience for each lead, and accelerate their progression through the funnel towards a successful sale.

Bottom of Funnel (BOFU) Techniques

The bottom of the funnel (BOFU) refers to the final stages of the customer journey, where leads are ready to make a purchase decision and become customers. At this stage, the goal of sales and marketing is to remove any remaining barriers or objections, create a sense of urgency and scarcity, and guide leads towards a successful close.

Here are some effective BOFU techniques for tech-powered sales teams:

Sales Demos and Trials: Offering personalized product demonstrations or free trials that allow potential buyers to experience the value and benefits of your solution firsthand. This can help to build trust and confidence in your product, and to address any specific questions or concerns that buyers may have. By using demo and trial management tools and analytics, you can streamline the scheduling and delivery of demos and trials, track user engagement and feedback, and identify opportunities for improvement and upselling.

Proposal and Quote Management: Creating and delivering professional and compelling proposals and quotes that clearly communicate the value and ROI of your solution, and make it easy for buyers to understand and compare their options. This can include using templates, pricing calculators, and e-signature tools to streamline the proposal creation and approval process, and to reduce friction and delays in the sales cycle. By using proposal and quote management platforms and analytics, you can track the performance and effectiveness of your proposals, and identify areas for optimization and improvement.

Negotiation and Closing Techniques: Employing proven negotiation and closing techniques that help to overcome objections, build urgency and commitment, and secure the sale. This can include using social proof, scarcity tactics, and risk-reversal offers to increase the perceived value and reduce the perceived risk of your solution. It can also include using collaborative negotiation strategies and win-win approaches to find mutually beneficial solutions and build long-term partnerships with customers. By using negotiation and closing tools and training, sales reps can improve their skills and confidence, and increase their win rates and deal sizes.

Customer Onboarding and Support: Providing a seamless and personalized onboarding and support experience that helps new customers to quickly realize the value and benefits of your solution, and to become successful and loyal users. This can include using onboarding and training platforms, knowledge bases, and support ticketing systems to streamline the customer education and issue resolution process, and to proactively identify and address any potential roadblocks or challenges. By using customer success and support analytics, you can track customer health and satisfaction, and identify opportunities for expansion and advocacy.

Referral and Advocacy Programs: Leveraging the power of customer referrals and advocacy to generate new leads and sales opportunities, and to build brand awareness and loyalty. This can include creating and promoting referral programs that incentivize customers to refer their colleagues and peers, and advocacy programs that recognize and reward customers for their public endorsements and testimonials. By using referral and advocacy marketing platforms and analytics, you can track the performance and ROI of your programs, and identify your most valuable and influential customers.

To optimize your BOFU techniques, it's important to align them with your sales process and customer success strategy, and to continuously monitor and analyze their performance and impact. Some key metrics to track include demo and trial conversion rates, proposal and quote win rates, negotiation and closing cycle times, customer onboarding and support satisfaction, and referral and advocacy program participation and revenue.

By using technology and data to inform and optimize your BOFU techniques, you can create a more efficient and effective sales process, and drive more predictable and profitable growth for your business.

Utilizing Behavioral AI for Lead Scoring

Lead scoring is a critical process for sales and marketing teams, as it helps to prioritize and route leads based on their likelihood to convert into customers. Traditionally, lead scoring has been based on demographic and firmographic attributes, such as job title, company size, and industry. However, these attributes alone may not provide a complete or accurate picture of a lead's readiness to buy, or their fit for your product or service.

This is where behavioral AI comes in. Behavioral AI is a type of artificial intelligence that analyzes and predicts human behavior, based on data from various sources such as web and mobile app usage, email and chat interactions, and social media activity. By applying behavioral AI to lead scoring, sales and marketing teams can gain a more comprehensive and dynamic understanding of each lead's interests, preferences, and intent, and adapt their engagement and nurturing strategies accordingly.

Here are some key benefits and applications of behavioral AI for lead scoring:

Real-Time Scoring and Prioritization: Behavioral AI can continuously monitor and analyze lead behavior across multiple channels and touchpoints, and update lead scores in real-time based on their actions and interactions. This can help sales and marketing teams to quickly identify and engage with the most promising and sales-ready leads, and to avoid wasting time and resources on lower-quality or unqualified leads.

Personalized and Relevant Engagement: Behavioral AI can provide insights into each lead's specific interests, pain points, and buying stage, and enable sales and marketing teams to deliver more personalized and relevant content and messaging. For example, if a lead has shown interest in a particular product feature or use case, behavioral AI can trigger a targeted email campaign or sales outreach that highlights the benefits and value of that feature for their specific needs and goals.

Predictive Modeling and Forecasting: Behavioral AI can use historical data and machine learning algorithms to build predictive models and forecasts of lead behavior and conversion likelihood. This can help sales and marketing teams to identify patterns and trends in lead behavior, and to anticipate and proactively address potential objections or roadblocks in the sales process. It can also help to improve demand planning and revenue forecasting, by providing more accurate and timely insights into the pipeline and funnel.

Sales and Marketing Alignment: Behavioral AI can provide a common language and framework for sales and marketing teams to collaborate and align around lead scoring and engagement. By using the same behavioral data and insights to inform their strategies and tactics, sales and marketing can create a more seamless and consistent experience for leads across the funnel, and avoid duplication or conflicting messaging. This can help to improve lead conversion rates, sales cycle times, and overall revenue growth.

To effectively implement behavioral AI for lead scoring, sales and marketing teams need to have access to high-quality and comprehensive data from across the customer journey, as well as the tools and platforms to collect, analyze, and act on that data in real-time. Some key considerations and best practices include:

- Identifying the key behavioral signals and triggers that indicate lead intent and readiness to buy, and mapping them to your lead scoring model and criteria.
- Integrating and normalizing data from multiple sources and systems, such as CRM, marketing automation, web analytics, and social media, to create a holistic view of each lead's behavior and engagement.
- Using machine learning and AI algorithms to continuously learn and optimize lead scoring models based on actual conversion and revenue data, and to detect and adapt to changes in lead behavior and market conditions.
- Providing sales and marketing teams with clear and actionable insights and recommendations based on lead scores and behavior, and enabling them to easily collaborate and coordinate their outreach and follow-up.

By leveraging behavioral AI for lead scoring, sales and marketing teams can create a more intelligent, personalized, and effective lead generation and nurturing process, and ultimately drive more revenue and growth for their business.

PART 5: EFFECTIVE SALES ENGAGEMENT

Multi-Channel Communication Strategies

In today's digital age, buyers are engaging with brands across multiple channels and devices, from email and social media to web and mobile apps. To effectively reach and engage these buyers, sales teams need to adopt a multi-channel communication strategy that leverages the strengths and synergies of each channel, and creates a seamless and consistent experience for the buyer.

Here are some key elements and best practices of a multi-channel sales communication strategy:

Channel Selection and Prioritization: The first step in developing a multi-channel strategy is to identify and prioritize the channels that are most relevant and effective for your target audience and sales process. This may include email, phone, social media, chat, video, and in-person meetings, among others. The choice of channels should be based on factors such as buyer preferences, industry norms, sales cycle length and complexity, and available resources and technology.

Messaging and Content Alignment: To create a consistent and compelling message across channels, sales teams need to align their messaging and content around a common set of themes, value propositions, and calls-to-action. This may involve developing a messaging framework or playbook that outlines the key talking points and proof points for each stage of the sales process and buyer journey. It may also involve creating and curating a library of content assets, such as case studies, whitepapers, demos, and proposals, that can be easily customized and repurposed for different channels and audiences.

Personalization and Relevance: To cut through the noise and capture the attention of busy buyers, sales teams need to personalize and tailor their outreach and engagement to the specific needs and interests of each individual or account. This may involve using data and insights from CRM, marketing automation, and other systems to segment and target buyers based on their demographics, behavior, and intent. It may also involve using AI and machine learning to dynamically generate and optimize content and offers based on real-time signals and feedback.

Timing and Cadence: To maximize the impact and efficiency of multi-channel outreach, sales teams need to carefully plan and orchestrate the timing and sequence of their communications across channels. This may involve using data and analytics to identify the optimal times and frequencies for each channel and buyer segment, based on factors such as response rates, conversion rates, and sales cycle velocity. It may also involve using automation and workflow tools to trigger and coordinate communications across channels based on buyer actions and milestones.

Measurement and Optimization: To continuously improve and optimize their multi-channel strategy, sales teams need to track and analyze key metrics and indicators across channels, such as open rates, click-through rates, response rates, meeting bookings, and revenue generated. This may involve using sales engagement and analytics platforms that provide a unified view of buyer interactions and outcomes across channels, and enable sales teams to test and refine their approaches based on data-driven insights.

By implementing a multi-channel communication strategy, sales teams can create a more engaging and effective sales process that meets buyers where they are, and guides them through the funnel with personalized and relevant interactions. Some examples and case studies of successful multi-channel sales strategies include:

- A SaaS company that uses a combination of email, social media, and targeted ads to attract and engage enterprise buyers, and then uses personalized demos and proposals to close deals and expand accounts.
- A financial services firm that uses a mix of phone, email, and chat to qualify and nurture leads, and then uses in-person meetings and events to build relationships and trust with high-value clients.
- A retail brand that uses social media and influencer partnerships to generate buzz and interest among millennial buyers, and then uses email and SMS to drive traffic and sales to their e-commerce site and mobile app.

Crafting Personalized Outreach

In a world of information overload and short attention spans, generic and impersonal sales outreach is no longer effective. To stand out and build rapport with buyers, sales teams need to craft personalized and relevant messages that demonstrate a deep understanding of the buyer's needs, challenges, and goals, and provide tangible value and insights.

Here are some key principles and techniques for crafting personalized sales outreach:

Research and Discovery: The foundation of personalized outreach is a thorough understanding of the buyer's context and situation. This requires sales reps to conduct research and gather insights from multiple sources, such as the buyer's company website, social media profiles, news and press releases, and industry reports. It also involves asking probing questions and actively listening to the buyer's responses, to uncover their pain points, priorities, and decision criteria.

Tailored Value Proposition: Based on the research and discovery, sales reps need to develop a tailored value proposition that clearly articulates how their product or service can help the buyer achieve their specific goals and overcome their specific challenges. This value proposition should be concise, compelling, and backed up by relevant data, examples, and customer testimonials. It should also be aligned with the buyer's industry, role, and stage in the buying process.

Personalized Content and Assets: To reinforce the value proposition and build credibility, sales reps need to provide personalized content and assets that are relevant and useful to the buyer. This may include customized demos, case studies, ROI calculators, and thought leadership pieces that showcase the rep's expertise and experience in the buyer's domain. It may also involve using dynamic content and data-driven personalization to tailor the messaging and offers to the buyer's specific interests and behaviors.

Authentic and Human Tone: To build trust and rapport, sales reps need to adopt an authentic and human tone in their outreach, rather than a formal or scripted one. This means using the buyer's name, referencing their specific situation and needs, and showing genuine interest and empathy. It also means avoiding sales jargon and buzzwords, and using clear and concise language that resonates with the buyer's communication style and preferences.

Multi-Channel and Multi-Touch: To maximize the impact and reach of personalized outreach, sales reps need to use a multi-channel and multi-touch approach that leverages the strengths and synergies of different channels and touchpoints. This may involve using email, phone, social media, and direct mail in a coordinated and sequential manner, based on the buyer's preferences and behaviors. It may also involve using automation and AI to scale and optimize the personalization across a large volume of buyers and interactions.

By crafting personalized outreach, sales teams can create a more engaging and effective sales process that builds trust, credibility, and loyalty with buyers. Some examples and case studies of successful personalized outreach include:

- A software company that uses AI and machine learning to analyze buyer data and generate personalized email and web content that highlights the specific benefits and use cases of their solution for each buyer.
- A consulting firm that uses account-based marketing and sales to develop customized value propositions and engagement plans for each target account, based on their industry, size, and strategic priorities.
- A travel agency that uses predictive analytics and recommendation engines to provide personalized travel suggestions and offers to each customer, based on their past bookings, preferences, and social media activity.

Using Conversational AI for Engagement

Conversational AI is a rapidly growing area of sales and marketing technology that uses natural language processing, machine learning, and other AI techniques to enable human-like interactions with customers across various channels and touchpoints. By automating and augmenting sales conversations, conversational AI can help sales teams to scale their outreach, improve their efficiency, and enhance their effectiveness in engaging and converting buyers.

Here are some key applications and benefits of conversational AI for sales engagement:

Chatbots and Virtual Assistants: Chatbots and virtual assistants are AI-powered software programs that can engage in natural language conversations with buyers across web, mobile, and messaging platforms. They can be used to answer common questions, provide product information and recommendations, and guide buyers through the sales process. By automating routine and repetitive tasks, chatbots and virtual assistants can free up sales reps to focus on more complex and high-value interactions, and provide 24/7 availability and responsiveness to buyer inquiries.

Personalized and Context-Aware Conversations: Conversational AI can use data and insights from CRM, marketing automation, and other systems to personalize and tailor the conversations to each buyer's specific needs, preferences, and context. For example, a chatbot can greet a returning visitor by name, reference their past interactions and purchases, and provide relevant and timely offers and recommendations based on their behavior and intent. By creating a more personalized and seamless experience across channels and touchpoints, conversational AI can improve buyer engagement, satisfaction, an d loyalty.

Sales Coaching and Enablement: Conversational AI can also be used to coach and enable sales reps to have more effective and productive conversations with buyers. For example, AI-powered tools can analyze sales call recordings and transcripts to identify best practices, common objections, and areas for improvement, and provide real-time guidance and suggestions to reps during live conversations. By leveraging machine learning and natural language processing, these tools can help sales reps to optimize their talk tracks, overcome obstacles, and close more deals.

Sentiment Analysis and Emotion Detection: Conversational AI can use advanced techniques such as sentiment analysis and emotion detection to understand and respond to the underlying emotions and attitudes of buyers during conversations. For example, a chatbot can detect when a buyer is frustrated or confused, and provide empathetic and helpful responses to address their concerns and build rapport. By recognizing and adapting to the emotional state of buyers, conversational AI can create a more human and engaging experience that builds trust and credibility.

Multilingual and Cross-Cultural Communication: Conversational AI can also enable sales teams to engage with buyers across different languages, cultures, and regions, by providing real-time translation and localization of conversations. For example, a virtual assistant can automatically detect the language and location of a buyer, and provide culturally appropriate greetings, expressions, and content that resonates with their specific context and preferences. By breaking down language and cultural barriers, conversational AI can help sales teams to expand their reach and penetrate new markets and segments.

To effectively implement conversational AI for sales engagement, sales teams need to have a clear strategy and roadmap that aligns with their overall sales goals and buyer journeys. They also need to have the right tools and platforms that can integrate with their existing systems and workflows, and provide a seamless and consistent experience across channels. Some key considerations and best practices include:

- Defining the use cases and scenarios where conversational AI can provide the most value and impact, such as lead qualification, product recommendations, and customer support.
- Designing and training the conversational AI models and scripts based on real buyer data and feedback, and continuously optimizing and refining them based on performance metrics and user input.
- Integrating conversational AI with other sales and marketing technologies, such as CRM, marketing automation, and sales enablement, to provide a holistic and data-driven view of the buyer journey and interactions.
- Providing sales reps with the training and support they need to effectively use and collaborate with conversational AI,

and to handle more complex and nuanced conversations that require human judgment and empathy.
- By leveraging conversational AI for sales engagement, sales teams can create a more intelligent, scalable, and human-centric sales process that drives more revenue and growth for their business. Some examples and case studies of successful conversational AI implementations include:
- A financial services company that uses a chatbot to provide personalized investment advice and recommendations to customers, based on their risk profile, goals, and portfolio performance.
- A healthcare provider that uses a virtual assistant to triage patient inquiries and symptoms, and to schedule appointments and follow-ups with the appropriate medical staff.
- An e-commerce retailer that uses a conversational AI platform to provide product recommendations, order tracking, and customer support across web, mobile, and social channels.

PART 6: OPTIMIZING SALES PROCESSES

Streamlining Sales Operations with Technology

Sales operations is a critical function that supports and enables the sales organization to perform at its best, by providing the processes, systems, and data that drive efficiency, effectiveness, and alignment. In today's fast-paced and complex sales environment, technology plays an increasingly important role in streamlining and optimizing sales operations, by automating manual tasks, improving data quality and accessibility, and providing real-time visibility and insights into sales performance.

Here are some key areas where technology can help to streamline sales operations:

Sales Process Automation: Technology can automate and standardize the sales process, from lead generation and qualification to opportunity management and forecasting. For example, sales force automation (SFA) tools can provide a central platform for managing and tracking sales activities, such as calls, emails, and meetings, and for enforcing best practices and compliance policies. By reducing manual data entry and errors, and providing a consistent and scalable process, sales process automation can improve the efficiency and productivity of sales reps, and reduce the time and cost of sales administration.

Data Management and Integration: Technology can help to manage and integrate the vast amounts of data that sales teams generate and consume, from customer and prospect information to market and competitive intelligence. For example, data management platforms (DMPs) can provide a single source of truth for sales data, by aggregating and cleansing data from multiple sources, such as CRM, marketing automation, and sales enablement systems. By providing a accurate and timely view of sales data, and enabling seamless data sharing and collaboration across teams and systems, data management and integration can improve the quality and usability of sales insights and analytics.

Sales Enablement and Content Management: Technology can help to enable and equip sales reps with the content, tools, and training they need to have effective and engaging conversations with buyers. For example, sales enablement platforms can provide a central repository and delivery mechanism for sales content, such as presentations, proposals, and case studies, and can track and measure the usage and impact of content on sales outcomes. By providing sales reps with easy access to relevant and up-to-date content, and enabling them to personalize and customize content for each buyer and situation, sales enablement and content management can improve the effectiveness and consistency of sales messaging and interactions.

Sales Performance Management: Technology can help to measure, analyze, and optimize sales performance, by providing real-time visibility and insights into key metrics and indicators, such as pipeline velocity, win rates, and quota attainment. For example, sales performance management (SPM) solutions can provide dashboards and reports that track and compare the performance of individual reps, teams, and regions, and can identify trends, gaps, and opportunities for improvement. By providing a data-driven and actionable view of sales performance, and enabling targeted coaching and training interventions, sales performance management can improve the motivation, accountability, and success of sales teams.

Sales Forecasting and Planning: Technology can help to forecast and plan sales revenue and resource allocation, by providing predictive and prescriptive analytics that model and simulate different scenarios and outcomes. For example, sales forecasting tools can use machine learning and statistical algorithms to predict future sales based on historical data, market trends, and external factors, and can provide confidence intervals and risk assessments for each forecast. By providing a more accurate and reliable view of future sales, and enabling data-driven decision making and resource allocation, sales forecasting and planning can improve the agility and resilience of sales organizations.

To effectively leverage technology for sales operations, sales leaders need to have a clear vision and roadmap for digital transformation, and a strong partnership and alignment with IT and other key stakeholders. They also need to have the right skills and capabilities to select, implement, and manage the appropriate technologies and solutions for their specific needs and goals. Some key considerations and best practices include:

- Assessing the current state of sales operations and identifying the key pain points, gaps, and opportunities for improvement that technology can address.
- Defining the future state of sales operations and the key capabilities and outcomes that technology can enable, such as increased productivity, better customer experience, and higher revenue growth.
- Developing a phased and iterative approach to technology adoption and implementation, that balances short-term quick wins with long-term strategic initiatives, and that involves key users and stakeholders in the design and testing process.
- Establishing governance and change management frameworks that ensure the ongoing alignment, adoption, and optimization of technology solutions, and that

measure and communicate the value and impact of technology on sales performance and business outcomes.
- By streamlining sales operations with technology, sales organizations can create a more agile, efficient, and data-driven sales engine that can adapt to changing market conditions and buyer expectations, and that can deliver sustainable and profitable growth. Some examples and case studies of successful sales operations transformations include:
- A global IT company that implemented a cloud-based CRM and sales enablement platform to standardize and automate its sales processes across regions and product lines, and to provide real-time visibility and collaboration for its distributed sales teams.
- A financial services firm that used advanced analytics and machine learning to predict and prioritize high-value sales opportunities, and to optimize its sales coverage and resource allocation based on data-driven insights and recommendations.
- A retail company that leveraged mobile and social technologies to enable its store associates to access customer data, product information, and sales tools on the go, and to provide personalized and seamless experiences for its shoppers across channels.

Implementing Sales Enablement Tools

Sales enablement is a strategic approach to empowering sales teams with the content, tools, and training they need to effectively engage buyers and drive revenue growth. In today's complex and competitive sales landscape, sales enablement tools play a critical role in improving the productivity, effectiveness, and alignment of sales teams, by providing them with the right resources and support at the right time and in the right context.

Here are some key types and benefits of sales enablement tools:

Content Management and Distribution: Sales enablement tools can help to centralize, organize, and distribute the vast amount of sales content that reps need to use in their conversations with buyers, such as presentations, case studies, and product demos. They can provide a single source of truth for sales content, and enable reps to easily search, filter, and access the most relevant and up-to-date content for each buyer and situation. They can also provide analytics and insights on content usage and effectiveness, and enable content creators to optimize and personalize content based on feedback and performance data.

Sales Training and Coaching: Sales enablement tools can help to onboard, train, and coach sales reps on the skills, knowledge, and behaviors they need to succeed in their roles. They can provide online and mobile learning modules, simulations, and assessments that enable reps to learn at their own pace and in their own style. They can also provide real-time guidance and feedback during sales conversations, using AI and machine learning to analyze call recordings and provide recommendations on how to handle objections, ask questions, and close deals. They can also enable managers to track and measure the progress and performance of their teams, and to provide targeted coaching and development based on individual needs and goals.

Sales Collaboration and Communication: Sales enablement tools can help to improve the collaboration and communication among sales reps, managers, and other key stakeholders, such as marketing, product, and customer success teams. They can provide social and mobile platforms that enable reps to share best practices, ask questions, and get help from their peers and experts. They can also provide integration with other sales and marketing systems, such as CRM, marketing automation, and content management, to enable seamless data sharing and workflow automation across the customer journey. They can also enable reps to communicate and engage with buyers across multiple channels, such as email, chat, and video, and to provide a consistent and personalized experience across touchpoints.

Sales Intelligence and Analytics: Sales enablement tools can help to provide sales teams with the data and insights they need to make informed decisions and improve their performance. They can integrate with various data sources, such as firmographic, technographic, and intent data providers, to provide a comprehensive view of each prospect and account, and to enable reps to tailor their outreach and messaging based on specific buyer needs and behaviors. They can also provide predictive and prescriptive analytics that can help reps to prioritize their activities, forecast their pipeline, and identify risks and opportunities in their deals. They can also provide benchmarking and comparison data that can help reps to understand their performance relative to their peers and industry standards, and to identify areas for improvement and growth.

To effectively implement sales enablement tools, sales leaders need to have a clear strategy and vision for how these tools can support and enhance their sales process and customer experience. They also need to have a strong partnership and alignment with other key functions, such as marketing, product, and IT, to ensure that the tools are integrated and optimized across the customer journey. Some key considerations and best practices for implementing sales enablement tools include:

Defining the Objectives and Metrics: Sales leaders need to define the specific objectives and metrics that they want to achieve with sales enablement tools, such as increasing win rates, reducing sales cycle times, or improving customer satisfaction. They also need to establish baseline measures and targets for these metrics, and to track and report on progress and results over time.

Assessing the Current State: Sales leaders need to assess the current state of their sales enablement capabilities and identify the gaps and opportunities for improvement. This may involve conducting surveys, interviews, and focus groups with sales reps, managers, and customers, to understand their needs, challenges, and expectations. It may also involve benchmarking their sales enablement maturity and performance against industry peers and best practices.

Selecting the Right Tools: Sales leaders need to select the right sales enablement tools that fit their specific needs and goals, based on factors such as ease of use, integration, scalability, and cost. They may need to evaluate and compare multiple vendors and solutions, and to involve key stakeholders and users in the selection process. They also need to ensure that the tools can adapt and evolve as their sales process and customer needs change over time.

Planning the Implementation: Sales leaders need to plan the implementation of sales enablement tools in a phased and iterative approach, that balances quick wins with long-term value. They need to define the scope, timeline, and resources required for each phase, and to identify the key milestones and deliverables. They also need to establish governance and change management frameworks that ensure the ongoing adoption, usage, and optimization of the tools, and that measure and communicate the value and impact of the tools on sales performance and customer experience.

Enabling the Users: Sales leaders need to enable and empower the users of sales enablement tools, by providing them with the training, support, and incentives they need to effectively use and benefit from the tools. This may involve conducting onboarding and certification programs, providing ongoing coaching and feedback, and recognizing and rewarding top performers and advocates. It may also involve establishing user communities and forums that enable reps to share best practices, ask questions, and provide feedback on the tools.

By implementing sales enablement tools, sales organizations can create a more productive, effective, and customer-centric sales force that can adapt to changing buyer expectations and market conditions. They can provide their reps with the content, skills, and insights they need to have more relevant, valuable, and personalized conversations with buyers, and to build trust and loyalty throughout the customer lifecycle. Some examples and case studies of successful sales enablement implementations include:

A global IT company that implemented a sales enablement platform to provide its reps with easy access to relevant and up-to-date content, and to enable them to personalize and customize their messaging and outreach based on buyer needs and behaviors. As a result, the company increased its content usage by 50%, reduced its sales cycle time by 20%, and improved its win rates by 15%.

A financial services firm that used a sales training and coaching tool to onboard and develop its new hires, and to provide ongoing skills and knowledge development for its experienced reps. The tool used AI and machine learning to analyze sales conversations and provide real-time feedback and guidance on how to improve performance. As a result, the firm reduced its onboarding time by 30%, increased its rep productivity by 25%, and improved its customer satisfaction scores by 20%.

A healthcare company that leveraged a sales intelligence and analytics platform to provide its reps with a 360-degree view of each account and prospect, and to enable them to prioritize their activities and forecast their pipeline based on data-driven insights and recommendations. The platform integrated with multiple data sources, such as CRM, marketing automation, and intent data providers, to provide a comprehensive and actionable view of each buyer and opportunity. As a result, the company increased its pipeline accuracy by 30%, reduced its sales cycle time by 25%, and improved its revenue growth by

20%.

Data-Driven Decision Making in Sales

Data-driven decision making is a critical capability for modern sales organizations that want to stay competitive and agile in a fast-changing market. By leveraging data and analytics to inform and guide their strategies, tactics, and operations, sales teams can make more accurate, timely, and effective decisions that drive better results and outcomes for their customers and their business.

Here are some key benefits and applications of data-driven decision making in sales:

Sales Forecasting and Planning: Data-driven decision making can help sales leaders to more accurately forecast and plan their revenue, pipeline, and resource requirements, based on historical trends, market indicators, and predictive models. By using data and analytics to identify patterns, correlations, and anomalies in their sales data, leaders can make more informed and confident decisions about where to invest their time, money, and talent, and how to optimize their sales coverage and territories. They can also use data to scenario-plan and stress-test their assumptions and risks, and to adjust their plans and targets based on changing conditions and opportunities.

Sales Performance Management: Data-driven decision making can help sales managers to more effectively measure, analyze, and improve the performance of their teams and individuals, based on key metrics and benchmarks. By using data and analytics to track and compare the activities, skills, and results of their reps, managers can identify top performers, best practices, and areas for improvement, and provide targeted coaching and development. They can also use data to set and adjust quotas, compensation, and incentives, and to motivate and retain high-performing reps. They can also use data to identify and address performance gaps and issues, such as pipeline leakage, low win rates, or long sales cycles, and to implement corrective actions and process improvements.

Customer Segmentation and Targeting: Data-driven decision making can help sales teams to more effectively segment and target their customers and prospects, based on their needs, behaviors, and value. By using data and analytics to create detailed profiles and personas of their ideal customers, sales teams can tailor their messaging, offerings, and engagement to the specific preferences and requirements of each segment. They can also use data to identify and prioritize high-value and high-potential accounts, and to allocate their resources and efforts accordingly. They can also use data to monitor and respond to changes in customer demand, sentiment, and loyalty, and to identify opportunities for cross-selling, upselling, and retention.

Sales Process Optimization: Data-driven decision making can help sales teams to continuously optimize and streamline their sales processes, based on data-driven insights and best practices. By using data and analytics to map and analyze the customer journey, sales teams can identify bottlenecks, inefficiencies, and opportunities for improvement, and implement changes and innovations that enhance the customer experience and accelerate the sales cycle. They can also use data to test and validate different sales methodologies, tools, and techniques, and to identify the most effective and efficient approaches for each stage of the sales process. They can also use data to monitor and measure the impact and ROI of their sales process improvements, and to make ongoing adjustments and refinements based on feedback and results.

To effectively implement data-driven decision making in sales, organizations need to have the right data, tools, and skills in place. They need to have access to accurate, complete, and timely data from multiple sources, such as CRM, marketing automation, sales enablement, and external providers. They need to have the tools and platforms to integrate, analyze, and visualize this data in meaningful and actionable ways, such as dashboards, reports, and predictive models. And they need to have the skills and capabilities to interpret, communicate, and act on the data-driven insights and recommendations, both at the leadership and the individual contributor levels.

Some key considerations and best practices for implementing data-driven decision making in sales include:

Defining the Data Strategy: Sales leaders need to define a clear and comprehensive data strategy that aligns with their business objectives and customer needs. They need to identify the key data sources, metrics, and use cases that will drive the most value and impact for their sales organization, and prioritize them based on feasibility, cost, and benefit. They also need to establish data governance and quality frameworks that ensure the consistency, security, and privacy of their sales data, and that enable them to comply with relevant regulations and standards.

Building the Data Infrastructure: Sales leaders need to build a robust and scalable data infrastructure that can support the collection, storage, processing, and analysis of large and diverse volumes of sales data. This may involve investing in cloud-based platforms, data warehouses, and analytics tools that can handle the speed, variety, and complexity of modern sales data. It may also involve partnering with IT and data science teams to design and implement the data architecture, pipelines, and models that enable real-time and predictive insights and actions.

Enabling the Data Culture: Sales leaders need to foster a data-driven culture that encourages and empowers sales teams to use data and analytics in their daily work and decision making. This may involve providing training and education on data literacy, visualization, and storytelling skills, and recognizing and rewarding data-driven behaviors and outcomes. It may also involve establishing feedback loops and collaboration channels that enable sales teams to share and discuss data-driven insights and best practices, and to provide input and suggestions on how to improve the data and analytics capabilities of the organization.

Measuring the Data Impact: Sales leaders need to measure and communicate the impact and value of data-driven decision making on sales performance and business outcomes. This may involve defining and tracking key performance indicators (KPIs) and return on investment (ROI) metrics that demonstrate the contribution and efficiency of data and analytics in driving revenue, margin, and customer satisfaction. It may also involve conducting regular reviews and assessments of the data and analytics initiatives, and making adjustments and optimizations based on feedback and results.

By embracing data-driven decision making, sales organizations can gain a significant competitive advantage in today's data-rich and dynamic market. They can make faster, smarter, and more customer-centric decisions that optimize their resources, processes, and performance, and that deliver superior value and experiences to their customers. Some examples and case studies of successful data-driven sales organizations include:

- A global technology company that used predictive analytics and machine learning to identify and prioritize high-value sales opportunities, and to provide real-time guidance and recommendations to sales reps on how to engage and convert these opportunities. As a result, the company increased its win rates by 30%, reduced its sales cycle time by 25%, and improved its customer lifetime value by 20%.
- A financial services firm that leveraged customer segmentation and behavior analytics to personalize and optimize its sales and marketing strategies for different customer groups and journeys. By using data to understand and anticipate the needs, preferences, and actions of each

segment, the firm was able to increase its cross-sell and upsell revenue by 40%, reduce its customer churn by 15%, and improve its net promoter score by 10 points.

- A healthcare company that used process mining and optimization techniques to identify and eliminate bottlenecks and inefficiencies in its sales and order management processes. By analyzing the flow and performance of each process step and activity, and simulating different scenarios and improvements, the company was able to reduce its order processing time by 50%, increase its order accuracy by 80%, and improve its customer satisfaction by 25%.

PART 7: SALES AUTOMATION AND AI

Automating Repetitive Tasks

Sales automation is a key enabler of modern, data-driven sales organizations that want to increase their efficiency, productivity, and agility in a fast-paced and competitive market. By using technology to automate repetitive and time-consuming tasks, sales teams can free up more time and resources to focus on high-value and strategic activities, such as building relationships, solving customer problems, and closing deals.

Here are some common examples of sales tasks that can be automated:

Lead Generation and Qualification: Sales teams can use automation tools to capture, enrich, and score leads from various sources, such as websites, social media, events, and referrals. These tools can use predefined criteria and algorithms to determine the quality and priority of each lead, and route them to the appropriate sales rep or queue for follow-up. They can also use progressive profiling and dynamic forms to gradually collect more information about each lead, and to personalize the content and messaging based on their interests and behaviors.

Email and Communication: Sales teams can use automation tools to create, schedule, and send personalized emails and other communications to prospects and customers at scale. These tools can use templates, variables, and conditional logic to tailor the content and timing of each message based on the recipient's profile, stage, and actions. They can also use AI-powered features, such as natural language processing and sentiment analysis, to optimize the subject lines, body copy, and calls-to-action for higher engagement and response rates.

Meeting and Task Scheduling: Sales teams can use automation tools to streamline the process of scheduling meetings and tasks with prospects, customers, and colleagues. These tools can integrate with calendar and scheduling apps to find available time slots, send invitations, and track confirmations and cancellations. They can also use AI-powered features, such as voice and text recognition, to automatically capture and summarize meeting notes and action items, and to update the relevant records and fields in the CRM system.

Data Entry and Management: Sales teams can use automation tools to reduce the manual effort and errors associated with data entry and management in the CRM and other sales systems. These tools can use APIs, web forms, and data connectors to automatically sync and update data from various sources, such as email, social media, and marketing automation platforms. They can also use data validation and enrichment features to ensure the accuracy and completeness of the data, and to fill in missing or outdated information from external databases and services.

Reporting and Analytics: Sales teams can use automation tools to generate and distribute reports and dashboards on key sales metrics and performance indicators, such as pipeline, revenue, and forecast. These tools can use predefined templates and filters to create customized and interactive reports for different audiences and purposes, such as executive summaries, team leaderboards, and individual scorecards. They can also use AI-powered features, such as anomaly detection and predictive modeling, to identify trends, risks, and opportunities in the sales data, and to provide actionable insights and recommendations.

To effectively implement sales automation, sales leaders need to have a clear understanding of their sales process, data, and technology landscape. They need to identify the tasks and activities that are most suitable and valuable for automation, based on factors such as frequency, complexity, and impact. They also need to select and integrate the right automation tools and platforms that can support their specific needs and goals, and that can scale and adapt as their business and market evolve.

Some key considerations and best practices for implementing sales automation include:

Defining the Automation Strategy: Sales leaders need to define a clear and compelling automation strategy that aligns with their overall sales strategy and customer experience vision. They need to articulate the key objectives, benefits, and metrics of automation, and how it will support and enhance the productivity, effectiveness, and satisfaction of their sales teams and customers. They also need to identify the key stakeholders, dependencies, and risks of automation, and develop a roadmap and governance model for its implementation and optimization.

Designing the Automation Workflows: Sales leaders need to design the automation workflows that will streamline and standardize the sales process and tasks. They need to map out the current state of their sales process, and identify the pain points, bottlenecks, and opportunities for improvement. They also need to define the future state of their sales process, and specify the inputs, outputs, and rules of each automated task and activity. They need to involve the sales teams and other key stakeholders in the design process, and gather their feedback and requirements to ensure the usability and adoption of the automation workflows.

Integrating the Automation Tools: Sales leaders need to select and integrate the automation tools and platforms that will enable and support the automation workflows. They need to evaluate and compare the features, capabilities, and costs of different automation solutions, and assess their compatibility and interoperability with their existing sales tech stack and data infrastructure. They also need to plan and execute the integration and configuration of the automation tools, and ensure the smooth and secure flow of data and actions across the different systems and channels.

Enabling the Automation Users: Sales leaders need to enable and empower the sales teams and other users of the automation tools. They need to provide the training, support, and incentives for the users to understand, adopt, and benefit from the automation workflows. They also need to establish the roles, responsibilities, and permissions for the users to access, use, and modify the automation tools and data. They need to monitor and measure the usage, performance, and impact of the automation tools, and gather the user feedback and suggestions for continuous improvement and optimization.

By automating repetitive tasks, sales organizations can achieve significant benefits, such as:

- Increased efficiency and productivity, by reducing the time and effort spent on manual and low-value tasks, and enabling sales reps to focus on more strategic and revenue-generating activities.
- Improved data quality and consistency, by reducing the errors and inconsistencies associated with manual data entry and management, and ensuring the accuracy and timeliness of the sales data and insights.
- Enhanced customer experience and engagement, by providing faster, more personalized, and more relevant interactions and communications with prospects and customers, and anticipating and addressing their needs

and preferences.
- Greater agility and scalability, by enabling sales teams to quickly adapt and respond to changing market conditions and opportunities, and to handle larger volumes and varieties of sales tasks and data.

Some examples and case studies of successful sales automation implementations include:

A software company that automated its lead generation and qualification process, by using web forms, chatbots, and AI-powered scoring and routing tools to capture and prioritize high-quality leads from its website and social media channels. As a result, the company increased its lead volume by 50%, reduced its lead response time by 80%, and improved its lead conversion rate by 30%.

A financial services firm that automated its email and communication process, by using personalized templates, dynamic content, and AI-powered optimization tools to create and send targeted and timely messages to its prospects and customers. As a result, the firm increased its email open and click-through rates by 40%, reduced its unsubscribe rate by 20%, and improved its customer satisfaction and loyalty scores by 25%.

A manufacturing company that automated its data entry and management process, by using APIs, web forms, and data validation and enrichment tools to automatically sync and update its sales data from various sources and systems. As a result, the company reduced its data entry time and errors by 90%, increased its data completeness and accuracy by 80%, and improved its sales forecast and pipeline visibility by 50%.

Enhancing Productivity with AI

Artificial intelligence (AI) is a transformative technology that is revolutionizing the way sales teams work and perform. By leveraging AI-powered tools and techniques, sales organizations can enhance their productivity, effectiveness, and intelligence in ways that were not possible before.

Here are some key applications and benefits of AI in sales:

Predictive Analytics and Forecasting: AI can help sales teams to accurately predict and forecast their sales performance and outcomes, based on historical data, market trends, and customer behaviors. By using machine learning algorithms and statistical models, AI can identify patterns, correlations, and anomalies in the sales data, and generate probabilistic estimates and confidence intervals for key metrics, such as revenue, pipeline, and quota attainment. This can help sales leaders to make data-driven decisions and plans, and to proactively manage risks and opportunities in their business.

Lead Scoring and Prioritization: AI can help sales teams to score and prioritize their leads based on their likelihood to convert and their potential value to the business. By using predictive models and behavioral analytics, AI can assess the quality and urgency of each lead, and assign them a score or rank based on factors such as demographics, firmographics, engagement, and intent. This can help sales reps to focus their time and effort on the most promising and profitable leads, and to personalize their outreach and messaging based on the lead's profile and stage.

Opportunity Insights and Recommendations: AI can help sales teams to gain deeper insights and recommendations on their sales opportunities, based on the historical performance and behavior of similar deals. By using machine learning algorithms and natural language processing, AI can analyze the characteristics, activities, and outcomes of past opportunities, and identify the key factors and actions that influence the win probability and deal size. This can help sales reps to optimize their sales process and tactics, and to receive real-time guidance and suggestions on how to advance and close each opportunity.

Conversation Intelligence and Coaching: AI can help sales teams to capture, analyze, and learn from their sales conversations and interactions with customers. By using speech recognition, sentiment analysis, and topic modeling, AI can transcribe and categorize the key moments, topics, and emotions in each conversation, and provide objective feedback and insights on the rep's performance and effectiveness. This can help sales managers to coach and develop their teams, and to identify the best practices and skills that drive successful outcomes.

Customer Engagement and Personalization: AI can help sales teams to engage and personalize their interactions with customers, based on their preferences, behaviors, and context. By using chatbots, virtual assistants, and recommendation engines, AI can provide 24/7 support and guidance to customers, and anticipate and address their needs and questions in real-time. This can help sales reps to build stronger relationships and loyalty with customers, and to cross-sell and upsell relevant products and services based on their interests and actions.

To effectively leverage AI in sales, organizations need to have a clear strategy and roadmap for AI adoption and implementation. They need to identify the key use cases and benefits of AI for their sales process and customer experience, and prioritize them based on their feasibility, impact, and alignment with their business goals. They also need to assess and address the technical, organizational, and cultural readiness and challenges of AI, and develop a change management and governance plan for its deployment and optimization.

Some key considerations and best practices for leveraging AI in sales include:

Defining the AI Vision and Objectives: Sales leaders need to define a clear and compelling vision and set of objectives for AI in sales, and communicate them to their teams and stakeholders. They need to articulate the key benefits and outcomes of AI, and how it will support and enhance the sales process, customer experience, and business performance. They also need to establish the key performance indicators (KPIs) and metrics for measuring and tracking the success and impact of AI initiatives.

Building the AI Data and Infrastructure: Sales leaders need to build a robust and scalable data and infrastructure foundation for AI in sales. They need to identify and integrate the key data sources and systems that will feed and support the AI models and applications, such as CRM, marketing automation, customer service, and external data providers. They also need to ensure the quality, security, and governance of the data, and establish the data management and analytics capabilities and processes for AI.

Selecting and Implementing the AI Solutions: Sales leaders need to select and implement the AI solutions and vendors that will enable and deliver the AI use cases and benefits. They need to evaluate and compare the features, capabilities, and costs of different AI solutions, and assess their fit and compatibility with their existing sales tech stack and data infrastructure. They also need to plan and execute the implementation and integration of the AI solutions, and ensure the smooth and secure flow of data and insights across the different systems and channels.

Enabling and Empowering the AI Users: Sales leaders need to enable and empower their sales teams and other users of the AI solutions. They need to provide the training, support, and incentives for the users to understand, adopt, and benefit from the AI tools an d insights. They also need to establish the roles, responsibilities, and permissions for the users to access, use, and modify the AI models and data. They need to monitor and measure the usage, performance, and impact of the AI solutions, and gather the user feedback and suggestions for continuous improvement and optimization.

By enhancing productivity with AI, sales organizations can

achieve significant benefits, such as:

- Increased sales efficiency and effectiveness, by automating and optimizing repetitive and complex tasks, and providing real-time guidance and recommendations to sales reps.
- Improved sales forecasting and pipeline management, by predicting and prioritizing the most promising and valuable opportunities, and identifying the key factors and actions that influence the win probability and deal size.
- Enhanced customer engagement and loyalty, by personalizing and contextualizing the interactions and communications with customers, and anticipating and addressing their needs and preferences in real-time.
- Greater sales agility and scalability, by enabling sales teams to quickly adapt and respond to changing market conditions and opportunities, and to handle larger volumes and varieties of sales data and activities.

Some examples and case studies of successful AI implementations in sales include:

A technology company that used AI-powered predictive analytics and forecasting to improve its sales planning and performance. By analyzing historical sales data, market trends, and customer behaviors, the AI solution generated accurate and granular forecasts for each sales rep, team, and region, and identified the key drivers and risks of the sales pipeline. As a result, the company increased its forecast accuracy by 20%, reduced its sales cycle time by 15%, and improved its revenue growth by 10%.

A financial services firm that used AI-powered lead scoring and prioritization to optimize its lead generation and qualification process. By analyzing the demographics, firmographics, engagement, and intent data of each lead, the AI solution assigned a score and rank to each lead, and recommended the best-fit products and offers for each lead. As a result, the firm increased its lead conversion rate by 30%, reduced its customer acquisition cost by 25%, and improved its sales productivity by 20%.

A healthcare company that used AI-powered conversation intelligence and coaching to enhance its sales training and development programs. By analyzing the sales calls and meetings of each rep, the AI solution identified the key moments, topics, and behaviors that influenced the call outcomes, and provided personalized feedback and coaching recommendations to each rep. As a result, the company increased its sales win rate by 25%, reduced its sales ramp-up time by 30%, and improved its customer satisfaction score by 15%.

Ethical Considerations in Sales Automation

As sales organizations increasingly adopt and rely on automation and AI technologies to enhance their productivity and performance, they also need to consider and address the ethical implications and risks of these technologies. Sales automation and AI can raise significant ethical concerns and challenges, such as:

Bias and Discrimination: AI models and algorithms can perpetuate and amplify the biases and discriminations that exist in the historical data and human judgments that they are trained on. This can lead to unfair and unequal treatment of certain customer segments or individuals, based on their demographic, socioeconomic, or behavioral characteristics. For example, an AI-powered lead scoring system may assign lower scores to leads from certain ethnic or geographic groups, based on the past performance and preferences of the sales team.

Privacy and Security: Sales automation and AI technologies often require the collection, storage, and analysis of large amounts of customer data, including personal and sensitive information. This can raise concerns about the privacy, security, and confidentiality of the data, and the potential for misuse, breach, or unauthorized access. For example, a chatbot or virtual assistant may accidentally reveal or share the personal details or conversation history of a customer with another user or system.

Transparency and Explainability: AI models and algorithms can be complex, opaque, and difficult to understand and interpret, even for the developers and users who create and deploy them. This can make it challenging to explain and justify the decisions and actions that are based on the AI insights and recommendations, and to ensure their transparency, accountability, and fairness. For example, a sales rep may not be able to explain why the AI system recommended a certain product or price to a customer, or how it arrived at that recommendation.

Human Agency and Autonomy: Sales automation and AI technologies can reduce or replace the need for human judgment, creativity, and empathy in the sales process. This can limit the ability of sales reps to make informed and independent decisions, and to adapt and respond to the unique needs and preferences of each customer. It can also create a sense of dependency and disempowerment among the sales teams, and reduce their motivation and engagement. For example, a sales rep may blindly follow the AI-generated script or playbook, without considering the context or feedback of the customer.

To address these ethical considerations and risks, sales organizations need to develop and implement a robust and responsible ethical framework and governance model for their sales automation and AI initiatives. Some key principles and best practices for ethical sales automation include:

Fairness and Non-Discrimination: Sales organizations should ensure that their AI models and algorithms are designed, trained, and tested to avoid and mitigate bias and discrimination, and to promote fairness and inclusivity. They should use diverse and representative data sets, and regularly monitor and audit the performance and outcomes of the AI systems for any disparate impacts or unintended consequences.

Privacy and Security: Sales organizations should implement strong privacy and security safeguards and policies for their customer data, and ensure compliance with relevant regulations and standards, such as GDPR, CCPA, and ISO 27001. They should obtain explicit consent from customers for the collection and use of their data, and provide them with clear and easy options to access, update, and delete their data.

Transparency and Explainability: Sales organizations should strive for transparency and explainability in their AI models and decisions, and provide clear and understandable information to customers and users about how the AI systems work and make recommendations. They should use interpretable and explainable AI techniques, such as rule-based systems, decision trees, and feature importance, and enable users to question, validate, and override the AI insights and actions.

Human Agency and Oversight: Sales organizations should empower and enable their sales teams to use their human judgment, creativity, and empathy in the sales process, and to collaborate with and complement the AI systems. They should provide training and support to the sales reps on how to interpret and apply the AI insights and recommendations, and how to adapt and personalize their approach based on the customer context and feedback. They should also establish human oversight and accountability mechanisms for the AI systems, and ensure that the final decisions and actions are made by humans, not machines.

By adopting and implementing an ethical framework and governance model for sales automation and AI, sales organizations can not only mitigate the risks and challenges of these technologies, but also enhance their trust, credibility, and reputation with customers, employees, and stakeholders. They can demonstrate their commitment to responsible and sustainable business practices, and differentiate themselves in an increasingly competitive and scrutinized market.

Some examples and case studies of ethical sales automation and AI initiatives include:

- A retail company that used an AI-powered personalization engine to recommend products and offers to customers, based on their browsing and purchase history. To ensure fairness and non-discrimination, the company used a diverse and representative data set to train the AI model, and regularly monitored and audited the recommendations for any biases or disparities. To ensure transparency and explainability, the company provided clear and concise explanations to customers about how the recommendations were generated, and enabled them to provide feedback and preferences.
- A financial services firm that used an AI-powered chatbot to provide customer support and guidance on its products and services. To ensure privacy and security, the firm implemented strong authentication, encryption, and access controls for the customer data, and obtained explicit consent from customers for the use of their data. To ensure human agency and oversight, the firm provided training and support to its customer service reps on how to monitor and intervene in the chatbot conversations, and escalate any complex or sensitive issues to human agents.
- A technology company that used an AI-powered sales forecasting and pipeline management system to predict and prioritize its sales opportunities. To ensure transparency and explainability, the company used interpretable and explainable AI techniques, such as decision trees and feature importance, to provide clear and understandable insights and recommendations to the sales reps. To ensure human agency and oversight, the company empowered and enabled the sales reps to use their judgment and expertise to validate and adjust the

AI predictions and actions, and to collaborate with the AI system to optimize the sales process and outcomes.

PART 8: SALES AND MARKETING ALIGNMENT

Creating a Unified Revenue Strategy

In today's complex and competitive business landscape, sales and marketing can no longer afford to operate in silos or pursue separate goals and strategies. To achieve sustainable and profitable growth, sales and marketing teams need to work together as one revenue team, with a unified vision, strategy, and execution plan.

A unified revenue strategy is a holistic and integrated approach that aligns the goals, metrics, and activities of sales and marketing around the customer journey and lifetime value. It recognizes that sales and marketing are two sides of the same coin, and that they need to collaborate and coordinate their efforts to attract, engage, convert, and retain customers.

Here are some key components and benefits of a unified revenue strategy:

Shared Goals and Metrics: A unified revenue strategy starts with defining and agreeing on the common goals and metrics that sales and marketing will pursue and measure. These goals and metrics should be based on the overall business objectives and customer needs, and should be specific, measurable, achievable, relevant, and time-bound (SMART). Some examples of shared goals and metrics include:By aligning their goals and metrics, sales and marketing can ensure that they are working towards the same outcomes, and can track and optimize their performance and impact.

- Revenue growth and profitability
- Customer acquisition and retention
- Lead generation and conversion
- Sales pipeline and velocity
- Customer satisfaction and loyalty

Integrated Planning and Execution: A unified revenue strategy requires sales and marketing to plan and execute their activities in a coordinated and integrated manner, across the entire customer lifecycle. This means that sales and marketing need to have a shared understanding and visibility of the customer journey, and need to collaborate and communicate regularly to ensure a seamless and consistent experience for the customer. Some examples of integrated planning and execution include:By planning and executing together, sales and marketing can leverage their strengths and resources, and deliver a more relevant and valuable experience to the customer.

- Joint account-based marketing (ABM) and account-based selling (ABS) programs
- Coordinated content and messaging across channels and touchpoints
- Aligned lead generation, qualification, and handoff processes
- Collaborative opportunity and deal management
- Integrated customer success and advocacy programs

Shared Data and Insights: A unified revenue strategy relies on sales and marketing having access to and using the same data and insights about the customer, the market, and the competition. This means that sales and marketing need to have a single source of truth for customer data, and need to share and analyze the data in real-time to inform their decisions and actions. Some examples of shared data and insights include:By sharing and leveraging data and insights, sales and marketing can gain a deeper understanding of the customer, and can adapt and optimize their strategies and tactics based on the changing needs and preferences of the customer.

- Customer demographics, firmographics, and behavioral data
- Lead scoring and prioritization models
- Opportunity and pipeline analytics
- Win/loss analysis and competitive intelligence
- Customer feedback and sentiment analysis

Aligned Incentives and Rewards: A unified revenue strategy requires sales and marketing to have aligned incentives and rewards that encourage and reinforce their collaboration and performance. This means that sales and marketing need to have shared and complementary compensation and recognition programs that reward them for achieving the common goals and metrics, and for supporting and enabling each other's success. Some examples of aligned incentives and rewards include:By aligning their incentives and rewards, sales and marketing can foster a culture of trust, respect, and accountability, and can motivate and engage their teams to work together towards the shared vision and goals.

- Revenue and profit-based commissions and bonuses
- Lead generation and conversion-based incentives
- Customer satisfaction and retention-based rewards
- Cross-functional team and individual recognition programs
- Career development and growth opportunities

To create and implement a unified revenue strategy, sales and marketing leaders need to have a strong partnership and commitment to change and innovation. They need to break down the silos and barriers that prevent sales and marketing from collaborating and communicating effectively, and need to establish the processes, tools, and governance models that enable and support their alignment and integration.

Some key steps and best practices for creating a unified revenue strategy include:

Defining the Vision and Objectives: Sales and marketing leaders need to define and articulate a clear and compelling vision and set of objectives for the unified revenue strategy, and communicate them to their teams and stakeholders. They need to ensure that the vision and objectives are aligned with the overall business strategy and customer needs, and are supported by the executive team and board.

Conducting a Gap Analysis: Sales and marketing leaders need to conduct a gap analysis to assess the current state of their alignment and integration, and identify the areas of improvement and opportunity. They need to review and benchmark their processes, systems, data, and metrics against the best practices and standards of their industry and peers, and prioritize the gaps and initiatives based on their impact and feasibility.

Developing the Roadmap and Plan: Sales and marketing leaders need to develop a roadmap and plan for implementing the unified revenue strategy, based on the gap analysis and prioritization. They need to define the key milestones, deliverables, and resources required for each initiative, and assign the roles and responsibilities for the implementation teams and stakeholders. They also need to establish the governance and change management frameworks for monitoring and optimizing the progress and outcomes of the initiatives.

Enabling the Teams and Technology: Sales and marketing leaders need to enable and empower their teams and technology to support and execute the unified revenue strategy. They need to provide the training, coaching, and support for their teams to develop the skills and mindsets required for collaboration and alignment, and to use the tools and systems that facilitate and automate their activities and communications. They also need to invest in and integrate the technology and data platforms that provide the single source of truth and real-time insights for the customer and revenue lifecycle.

By creating and implementing a unified revenue strategy, sales and marketing organizations can achieve significant benefits and competitive advantages, such as:

- Increased revenue growth and profitability, by aligning and optimizing the efforts and resources of sales and marketing around the customer journey and lifetime value.
- Improved customer acquisition and retention, by delivering a more consistent and personalized experience across the channels and touchpoints, and by leveraging the data and insights to anticipate and meet the changing needs and preferences of the customer.
- Enhanced sales and marketing efficiency and effectiveness, by reducing the duplication and waste of efforts and resources, and by leveraging the strengths and expertise of each function to support and enable the other.
- Greater agility and innovation, by fostering a culture of collaboration, experimentation, and learning, and by adapting and responding faster to the changes and disruptions in the market and customer landscape.

Some examples and case studies of successful unified revenue strategies include:

- A technology company that implemented an account-based marketing and selling program to align its sales and marketing teams around the key accounts and opportunities. The program involved creating joint account plans, developing personalized content and messaging, and coordinating the outreach and engagement across the channels and touchpoints. As a result, the company

increased its account win rate by 30%, reduced its sales cycle time by 20%, and improved its customer retention rate by 15%.
- A financial services firm that established a revenue operations function to integrate and optimize its sales and marketing processes, systems, and data. The function was responsible for defining and managing the lead generation, qualification, and handoff processes, and for providing the analytics and insights to inform the sales and marketing strategies and tactics. As a result, the firm increased its lead conversion rate by 25%, reduced its customer acquisition cost by 20%, and improved its sales productivity by 15%.
- A healthcare company that created a customer success and advocacy program to align its sales and marketing teams around the post-sale customer experience and loyalty. The program involved defining and measuring the customer health and satisfaction metrics, and providing the training, support, and rewards for the sales and marketing teams to retain and grow the customer relationships. As a result, the company increased its customer retention rate by 20%, improved its Net Promoter Score by 10 points, and increased its cross-sell and upsell revenue by 15%.

Content-Driven Demand Generation

Content is one of the most powerful and effective tools for driving demand generation and customer engagement in today's digital and information-rich world. By creating and distributing valuable, relevant, and consistent content that addresses the needs, interests, and challenges of the target audience, sales and marketing teams can attract, educate, and nurture potential customers, and guide them through the buying journey.

Content-driven demand generation is a strategic approach that leverages content as the primary driver and enabler of the demand generation process, from awareness to consideration to decision. It involves developing and executing a content strategy that is aligned with the buyer personas, journey stages, and objectives, and that provides the right content, to the right audience, at the right time, and in the right format.

Here are some key components and benefits of content-driven demand generation:

Buyer Persona and Journey Mapping: Content-driven demand generation starts with a deep understanding and mapping of the buyer personas and journey stages. Buyer personas are fictional representations of the ideal customers, based on their demographics, behaviors, goals, and challenges. Journey stages are the different phases that the buyer goes through, from awareness to consideration to decision to loyalty. By developing and aligning the content with the buyer personas and journey stages, sales and marketing teams can ensure that the content is relevant, personalized, and timely, and can guide the buyer towards the desired action and outcome.

Content Planning and Development: Content-driven demand generation requires a strategic and systematic approach to content planning and development. This involves defining the content themes, topics, formats, and channels that are most effective and engaging for the target audience, and creating a content calendar and workflow that ensures the consistency, quality, and timeliness of the content. Some examples of content types and formats for demand generation include:By developing a diverse and compelling mix of content, sales and marketing teams can cater to the different preferences and needs of the buyer personas, and can provide a rich and immersive experience that educates, entertains, and engages the audience.

- Blog posts and articles
- E-books and whitepapers
- Infographics and visual content
- Videos and webinars
- Case studies and testimonials

- Social media and email content

Content Distribution and Promotion: Content-driven demand generation requires a multi-channel and integrated approach to content distribution and promotion. This involves leveraging the owned, earned, and paid media channels to reach and engage the target audience, and to amplify the reach and impact of the content. Some examples of content distribution and promotion channels include:By distributing and promoting the content through the right channels and tactics, sales and marketing teams can increase the visibility, credibility, and authority of the brand, and can drive more traffic, leads, and conversions to the website and sales funnel.

- Company website and blog
- Social media platforms
- Email marketing and newsletters
- Paid advertising and sponsorships
- Influencer and partner marketing
- PR and media relations

Content Performance and Optimization: Content-driven demand generation requires a data-driven and continuous approach to content performance and optimization. This involves measuring and analyzing the key metrics and indicators of content effectiveness and engagement, such as:By tracking and optimizing the content performance metrics, sales and marketing teams can identify the best-performing and highest-converting content pieces and formats, and can refine and improve the content strategy and execution based on the insights and feedback.

- Website traffic and pageviews
- Social media shares and likes
- Email opens and clicks
- Lead generation and conversion rates
- Sales pipeline and revenue attribution

To create and implement a content-driven demand generation strategy, sales and marketing leaders need to have a strong collaboration and alignment around the content vision, goals, and metrics. They need to establish the processes, tools, and governance models that enable and support the content creation, distribution, and optimization, and need to foster a culture of experimentation, learning, and innovation.

Some key steps and best practices for creating a content-driven demand generation strategy include:

Conducting a Content Audit and Gap Analysis: Sales and marketing leaders need to conduct a content audit and gap analysis to assess the current state and effectiveness of their content assets and initiatives, and to identify the areas of improvement and opportunity. They need to review and evaluate the content themes, topics, formats, and channels against the buyer personas and journey stages, and prioritize the gaps and initiatives based on their impact and feasibility.

Developing the Content Strategy and Plan: Sales and marketing leaders need to develop a content strategy and plan based on the audit and gap analysis. They need to define the content vision, goals, and metrics that are aligned with the overall demand generation and business objectives, and to create a content calendar and workflow that outlines the content pieces, formats, channels, and timelines. They also need to assign the roles and responsibilities for the content creation, review, and approval, and to establish the governance and change management frameworks for monitoring and optimizing the content performance and outcomes.

Enabling the Content Teams and Technology: Sales and marketing leaders need to enable and empower their content teams and technology to support and execute the content-driven demand generation strategy. They need to provide the training, coaching, and support for their teams to develop the skills and mindsets required for content creation, curation, and promotion, and to use the tools and systems that facilitate and automate the content workflows and analytics. They also need to invest in and integrate the content management, marketing automation, and analytics platforms that provide the single source of truth and real-time insights for the content lifecycle and performance.

Measuring and Optimizing the Content Impact: Sales and marketing leaders need to measure and optimize the content impact and ROI on a regular and ongoing basis. They need to define and track the key performance indicators (KPIs) and metrics that are aligned with the content goals and objectives, and to analyze and report on the content effectiveness and engagement across the channels and touchpoints. They also need to gather and incorporate the feedback and insights from the target audience, sales teams, and other stakeholders, and to continuously refine and improve the content strategy and execution based on the data and learning.

By creating and implementing a content-driven demand generation strategy, sales and marketing organizations can achieve significant benefits and competitive advantages, such as:

- Increased brand awareness and thought leadership, by providing valuable and insightful content that educates and inspires the target audience, and that positions the brand as a trusted and credible source of information and expertise.
- Improved lead generation and nurturing, by attracting and engaging the right prospects with the right content at the right time, and by guiding them through the buying journey with personalized and relevant content experiences.
- Enhanced sales enablement and acceleration, by providing the sales teams with the content assets and insights that

help them to understand and address the buyer needs and objections, and to accelerate the sales cycle and win rates.
- Greater customer engagement and loyalty, by delivering consistent and valuable content experiences that educate, entertain, and delight the customers, and that foster long-term relationships and advocacy.

Some examples and case studies of successful content-driven demand generation strategies include:

A software company that created a series of educational and thought-provoking e-books and webinars that addressed the key challenges and trends in their industry, and that provided practical and actionable advice and best practices. The company promoted the content through their website, social media, email, and paid channels, and used progressive profiling and lead scoring to qualify and nurture the leads. As a result, the company increased their lead generation by 50%, reduced their cost per lead by 30%, and improved their lead-to-customer conversion rate by 20%.

A financial services firm that developed a content hub and newsletter that curated and shared the latest news, insights, and opinions on the financial markets and investment strategies. The firm partnered with industry influencers and experts to create and contribute to the content, and used social media and email to distribute and promote the content to their target audience. As a result, the firm increased their website traffic by 200%, grew their email subscriber base by 150%, and generated 50% more sales opportunities from the content.

A healthcare company that created a series of patient success stories and testimonial videos that showcased the real-life impact and benefits of their products and services. The company used social media and paid advertising to target and reach the specific patient segments and personas, and used marketing automation to nurture and convert the leads with personalized content and offers. As a result, the company increased their brand awareness and consideration by 30%, improved their lead quality and conversion rate by 25%, and increased their customer retention and referral rate by 15%.

Measuring and Optimizing Marketing Impact on Sales

Measuring and optimizing the impact of marketing on sales is a critical and ongoing process for any organization that wants to drive growth, efficiency, and competitive advantage. By tracking and analyzing the key metrics and indicators of marketing performance and contribution to revenue, sales and marketing leaders can gain visibility and insights into what's working, what's not, and where to focus their efforts and resources for maximum impact and ROI.

However, measuring and optimizing marketing impact on sales is not a simple or straightforward task, as it involves multiple variables, channels, and stakeholders, and requires a holistic and integrated approach to data, analytics, and decision-making. Sales and marketing leaders need to have a clear and shared understanding of the goals, metrics, and attribution models that define and quantify the marketing impact on sales, and need to establish the processes, tools, and governance frameworks that enable and support the continuous measurement and optimization of marketing performance.

Here are some key components and benefits of measuring and optimizing marketing impact on sales:

Defining the Goals and Metrics: The first step in measuring and optimizing marketing impact on sales is to define the goals and metrics that align with the overall business objectives and revenue targets. Sales and marketing leaders need to agree on the specific outcomes and indicators that marketing should drive and contribute to, such as:By defining and tracking the right goals and metrics, sales and marketing leaders can ensure that they are focusing on the most impactful and relevant areas of marketing performance, and can align their strategies and tactics accordingly.

- Lead generation and qualification
- Pipeline creation and acceleration
- Revenue and bookings attribution
- Customer acquisition and retention
- Brand awareness and consideration

Establishing the Attribution Models: The next step is to establish the attribution models that determine how marketing activities and touchpoints are credited and weighted for their contribution to sales and revenue. Attribution models can range from simple and rule-based, such as first-touch or last-touch, to more complex and data-driven, such as multi-touch or algorithmic. Sales and marketing leaders need to choose the attribution models that best reflect the customer journey and buying process, and that provide the most accurate and actionable insights into the marketing impact on sales. Some examples of attribution models include:By establishing the right attribution models, sales and marketing leaders can gain a more granular and nuanced understanding of how different marketing activities and channels influence and drive sales and revenue, and can optimize their investments and allocations accordingly.

- First-touch attribution: Credits 100% of the revenue to the first marketing touchpoint that generated the lead or opportunity.
- Last-touch attribution: Credits 100% of the revenue to the last marketing touchpoint that preceded the sale or conversion.
- Linear attribution: Distributes the revenue equally across all marketing touchpoints that influenced the sale or conversion.
- Time-decay attribution: Assigns more credit to the marketing touchpoints that occurred closer to the sale or

conversion, based on a decaying time window.
- Position-based attribution: Assigns a fixed percentage of credit to the first and last touchpoints, and distributes the remaining credit equally across the middle touchpoints.
- Data-driven attribution: Uses machine learning and statistical models to dynamically assign credit to the marketing touchpoints based on their relative impact and contribution to the sale or conversion.

Implementing the Measurement and Reporting Systems: To effectively measure and optimize marketing impact on sales, organizations need to have the right data, tools, and processes in place. This involves implementing the marketing measurement and reporting systems that can capture, integrate, and analyze the data from multiple sources and channels, such as:Sales and marketing leaders need to ensure that the data is accurate, complete, and timely, and that it is unified and normalized across the different systems and touchpoints. They also need to establish the dashboards, reports, and alerts that provide the real-time and actionable insights into the marketing performance and impact on sales, and that enable the teams to monitor, diagnose, and optimize their activities and results.

- CRM and sales force automation platforms
- Marketing automation and email platforms
- Web and mobile analytics platforms
- Social media and advertising platforms
- Customer service and support platforms

Optimizing and Iterating the Marketing Strategies and Tactics: The ultimate goal of measuring and optimizing marketing impact on sales is to drive continuous improvement and innovation in the marketing strategies and tactics. By analyzing the data and insights from the measurement and reporting systems, sales and marketing leaders can identify the areas of strength, weakness, and opportunity in their marketing programs and campaigns, and can make informed and data-driven decisions to optimize and iterate their approaches. Some examples of optimization and iteration opportunities include:By continuously optimizing and iterating the marketing strategies and tactics based on the data and insights, sales and marketing leaders can drive more effective, efficient, and customer-centric marketing programs that deliver measurable and sustainable impact on sales and revenue growth.

- A/B testing and multivariate testing of different marketing messages, offers, and creative elements, to identify the most effective and engaging versions for different segments and channels.
- Predictive modeling and scoring of the most promising and valuable leads and opportunities, based on their demographic, behavioral, and engagement data, to prioritize and personalize the sales and marketing outreach and follow-up.
- Attribution analysis and reporting of the most impactful and efficient marketing touchpoints and channels, based on their contribution and ROI to the sales and revenue pipeline, to optimize the budget and resource allocation and mix.
- Customer journey mapping and optimization of the most common and critical paths and stages that customers take from awareness to consideration to purchase to loyalty, based on their feedback, behavior, and sentiment data, to identify and remove the friction points and gaps in the marketing and sales experience.

To successfully measure and optimize marketing impact on sales, organizations need to have a strong culture of data-driven decision-making, experimentation, and collaboration across the sales and marketing functions. They need to break down the silos and barriers that prevent the sharing and leveraging of data, insights, and best practices, and need to establish the processes, incentives, and governance models that enable and reward the continuous improvement and innovation of marketing performance and impact.

Some key steps and best practices for measuring and optimizing marketing impact on sales include:

Aligning the Sales and Marketing Goals and Metrics: Sales and marketing leaders need to align and agree on the specific goals and metrics that define and quantify the marketing impact on sales, and that are aligned with the overall business objectives and revenue targets. They need to establish a shared language and framework for measuring and reporting on marketing performance, and need to ensure that the goals and metrics are specific, measurable, achievable, relevant, and time-bound (SMART).

Implementing the Marketing Measurement and Reporting Systems: Sales and marketing leaders need to implement and integrate the marketing measurement and reporting systems that can capture, analyze, and visualize the data from multiple sources and channels, and that provide the real-time and actionable insights into the marketing performance and impact on sales. They need to ensure that the data is accurate, complete, and timely, and that it is unified and normalized across the different systems and touchpoints. They also need to establish the dashboards, reports, and alerts that enable the teams to monitor, diagnose, and optimize their activities and results.

Establishing the Attribution Models and Frameworks: Sales and marketing leaders need to establish and agree on the attribution models and frameworks that determine how marketing activities and touchpoints are credited and weighted for their contribution to sales and revenue. They need to choose the attribution models that best reflect the customer journey and buying process, and that provide the most accurate and actionable insights into the marketing impact on sales. They also need to ensure that the attribution models are consistent, transparent, and fair across the different channels and touchpoints, and that they are regularly reviewed and updated based on the data and feedback.

Optimizing and Iterating the Marketing Strategies and Tactics: Sales and marketing leaders need to continuously optimize and iterate the marketing strategies and tactics based on the data and insights from the measurement and reporting systems. They need to identify the areas of strength, weakness, and opportunity in their marketing programs and campaigns, and need to make informed and data-driven decisions to improve and innovate their approaches. They also need to establish the processes, incentives, and governance models that enable and reward the experimentation, learning, and collaboration across the sales and marketing teams, and that drive the continuous improvement and impact of marketing performance on sales and revenue growth.

By effectively measuring and optimizing marketing impact on sales, organizations can achieve significant benefits and competitive advantages, such as:

- Increased visibility and accountability of marketing performance and contribution to revenue, by establishing clear and measurable goals, metrics, and attribution models that quantify and demonstrate the impact and ROI of marketing on sales and business outcomes.
- Improved efficiency and effectiveness of marketing investments and resources, by optimizing and allocating the marketing budget and mix based on the data and insights from the measurement and reporting systems, and by focusing on the most impactful and efficient channels, tactics, and segments.
- Enhanced alignment and collaboration between sales and marketing functions, by establishing a shared language, framework, and process for measuring and optimizing marketing impact on sales, and by fostering a culture of data-driven decision-making, experimentation, and continuous improvement across the teams.

- Greater agility and innovation in marketing strategies and tactics, by leveraging the data and insights from the measurement and reporting systems to identify and test new ideas, approaches, and technologies that can drive more effective and differentiated marketing programs and campaigns, and that can adapt and respond to the changing customer needs and market conditions.

Some examples and case studies of successful measurement and optimization of marketing impact on sales include:

- A technology company that implemented a multi-touch attribution model and reporting system to measure and optimize the impact and ROI of their digital marketing programs on lead generation, pipeline creation, and revenue bookings. The company used the data and insights from the attribution model to identify the most effective and efficient channels, tactics, and content for different segments and stages of the customer journey, and to optimize their budget and resource allocation accordingly. As a result, the company increased their marketing-sourced pipeline by 50%, improved their marketing ROI by 30%, and accelerated their sales cycle by 20%.
- A financial services firm that established a customer journey mapping and optimization framework to measure and optimize the impact and experience of their marketing and sales touchpoints on customer acquisition, retention, and loyalty. The firm used the data and insights from the customer journey mapping to identify the most common and critical paths and stages that customers took from awareness to consideration to purchase to advocacy, and to optimize and personalize their marketing and sales strategies and tactics accordingly. As a result, the firm increased their customer acquisition rate by 25%, improved their customer retention rate by 15%, and grew their customer lifetime value by 20%.
- A healthcare company that implemented a predictive

lead scoring and prioritization system to measure and optimize the impact and efficiency of their marketing lead generation and qualification programs on sales pipeline and revenue. The company used machine learning and predictive analytics to score and rank their leads based on their demographic, behavioral, and engagement data, and to prioritize and route their leads to the most appropriate sales teams and reps for follow-up and conversion. As a result, the company increased their lead-to-opportunity conversion rate by 40%, improved their sales productivity by 30%, and grew their marketing-sourced revenue by 50%.

PART 9: CASE STUDIES AND REAL-LIFE APPLICATIONS

Success Stories from Tech-Powered Sales Leaders

Tech-powered sales is not just a theory or a vision; it is a reality and a necessity for many organizations that want to stay competitive and grow in today's digital and data-driven world. Across industries and regions, there are numerous examples and success stories of sales leaders and teams that have embraced and leveraged technology to transform and optimize their sales processes, strategies, and results.

Here are some inspiring and insightful success stories from tech-powered sales leaders:

Salesforce: Salesforce is not just a leading provider of sales and marketing technology; it is also a pioneer and practitioner of tech-powered sales. Salesforce has built a data-driven and customer-centric sales culture that leverages its own platform and tools to drive growth, efficiency, and innovation. Some of the key elements of Salesforce's tech-powered sales approach include:As a result of its tech-powered sales approach, Salesforce has achieved impressive growth and customer success outcomes, such as:

- A single source of truth for customer data and interactions, powered by Salesforce CRM and integrated with multiple

systems and channels.
- A data-driven and AI-powered lead scoring and routing system that prioritizes and assigns leads based on their fit, intent, and behavior.
- A personalized and multi-channel sales engagement strategy that leverages email, phone, social, and video to build relationships and trust with customers.
- A collaborative and transparent sales forecasting and pipeline management process that uses Einstein Analytics and AI to predict and optimize revenue outcomes.
- A continuous learning and coaching culture that uses Salesforce's own training and enablement tools to upskill and empower sales reps and managers.
- Consistently high revenue growth rates, averaging over 25% year-over-year for the past decade.
- Industry-leading customer satisfaction and loyalty scores, with an average customer satisfaction score of 4.7 out of 5 and a customer retention rate of over 90%.
- A highly productive and engaged sales force, with an average sales productivity of over $1 million per rep and a sales employee satisfaction score of over 90%.

Microsoft: Microsoft is another tech giant that has transformed its sales organization and culture through technology and data. Microsoft has shifted from a product-centric and transactional sales model to a customer-centric and solution-oriented sales approach that leverages its own cloud and AI platforms to drive value and outcomes for customers. Some of the key elements of Microsoft's tech-powered sales approach include:As a result of its tech-powered sales approach, Microsoft has achieved significant growth and customer impact outcomes, such as:

- A customer insights and intelligence platform that aggregates and analyzes data from multiple sources, such as CRM, marketing automation, social media, and third-party providers, to create a 360-degree view of each customer and their needs, preferences, and behaviors.

- A solution-oriented and value-based sales process that uses Microsoft's own industry and domain expertise, as well as its cloud and AI solutions, to identify and solve customer challenges and opportunities.
- A digital and self-service sales motion that enables customers to explore, evaluate, and purchase Microsoft products and services online, with the support and guidance of virtual agents and chatbots.
- A data-driven and agile sales planning and execution process that uses machine learning and predictive analytics to optimize territory design, quota setting, and resource allocation.
- A continuous learning and innovation culture that uses Microsoft's own sales academy and enablement resources to develop and retain top sales talent, and to foster creativity and experimentation.
- Double-digit revenue growth rates in its commercial cloud and enterprise businesses, driven by the adoption and expansion of its Azure, Office 365, and Dynamics 365 platforms.
- High customer satisfaction and advocacy scores, with an average Net Promoter Score of over 50 and a customer referral rate of over 80%.
- A diverse and inclusive sales force, with over 40% of its sales leadership roles held by women and underrepresented minorities, and a sales employee engagement score of over 90%.

Amazon Web Services (AWS): AWS is the market leader in cloud computing and a pioneer in tech-powered sales and customer success. AWS has built a customer-obsessed and data-driven sales culture that leverages its own cloud and machine learning services to deliver value and innovation to customers. Some of the key elements of AWS's tech-powered sales approach include:As a result of its tech-powered sales approach, AWS has achieved remarkable growth and customer success outcomes, such as:

- A customer-centric and solution-oriented sales process that uses AWS's own industry and domain expertise, as well as its cloud and machine learning solutions, to identify and solve customer challenges and opportunities.
- A data-driven and personalized sales engagement strategy that uses AWS's own customer intelligence and recommendation engines to tailor and optimize the messaging, content, and offers for each customer and their stage in the buying journey.
- A collaborative and agile sales and solution architecture team that works closely with customers to design, implement, and optimize their cloud solutions and outcomes, using AWS's own best practices and frameworks.
- A continuous learning and innovation culture that uses AWS's own sales enablement and certification programs to develop and empower sales reps and managers, and to foster a growth mindset and customer obsession.
- Consistently high revenue growth rates, averaging over 40% year-over-year for the past decade, and reaching over $40 billion in annual revenue in 2020.
- Industry-leading customer satisfaction and loyalty scores, with an average customer satisfaction score of over 90% and a customer retention rate of over 95%.
- A highly skilled and customer-centric sales force, with over 80% of its sales reps holding at least one AWS certification, and a sales employee engagement score of over 90%.

These success stories demonstrate the power and potential of tech-powered sales in driving growth, efficiency, and customer value. They also highlight some of the key elements and best practices of a tech-powered sales approach, such as:

- A customer-centric and data-driven sales culture that leverages technology and analytics to understand and serve customer needs and preferences.

- A collaborative and agile sales process that uses cross-functional teams and iterative methods to design, deliver, and optimize customer solutions and outcomes.
- A continuous learning and innovation mindset that invests in sales enablement, coaching, and experimentation to develop and empower sales talent and performance.
- Sales leaders and teams can learn from and adapt these success stories to their own context and goals, and can use them as inspiration and guidance for their own tech-powered sales transformation and optimization journeys.

Practical Applications of AI in Sales

Artificial Intelligence (AI) is one of the most transformative and impactful technologies for sales today. AI has the potential to revolutionize and optimize every aspect of the sales process and experience, from prospecting and lead generation to forecasting and customer success. By leveraging the power of machine learning, natural language processing, and predictive analytics, sales teams can automate and augment their tasks and decisions, and can deliver more personalized, efficient, and effective customer interactions and outcomes.

Here are some of the most promising and practical applications of AI in sales:

Lead Generation and Qualification: AI can help sales teams to identify, attract, and qualify the most promising and profitable leads, based on their fit, intent, and engagement data. Some examples of AI-powered lead generation and qualification tools include:

- Predictive lead scoring models that use machine learning algorithms to analyze and rank leads based on their demographic, firmographic, behavioral, and technographic data, and to predict their likelihood to convert and their potential value.

- Chatbots and virtual assistants that use natural language processing and dialogue management to engage and qualify leads through conversational interfaces, and to route them to the most appropriate sales reps or resources based on their needs and preferences.
- Account-based marketing platforms that use AI to identify and target the most valuable and influential accounts and contacts, and to orchestrate personalized and multi-channel campaigns and experiences to engage and convert them.

Sales Forecasting and Pipeline Management: AI can help sales teams to accurately predict and manage their revenue and pipeline outcomes, based on their historical, real-time, and external data. Some examples of AI-powered sales forecasting and pipeline management tools include:

- Predictive forecasting models that use machine learning algorithms to analyze and forecast sales performance and outcomes, based on factors such as deal size, stage, age, and sentiment, and to provide early warning and optimization recommendations.
- Conversational intelligence platforms that use natural language processing and sentiment analysis to analyze and score sales conversations and interactions, and to provide insights and coaching on performance, objection handling, and closing techniques.
- Sales performance management systems that use AI to optimize and align sales planning, forecasting, and incentive compensation processes, and to provide real-time visibility and analytics on sales outcomes and trends.

Sales Enablement and Training: AI can help sales teams to access and apply the most relevant and effective knowledge, content, and skills, based on their context and needs. Some examples of AI-powered sales enablement and training tools include:

- Sales content management platforms that use AI to recommend and personalize the most relevant and engaging content and assets for each sales situation and buyer persona, and to track and optimize their usage and impact.
- Sales readiness and coaching platforms that use AI to assess and develop sales reps' skills and behaviors, through simulations, role-plays, and feedback, and to provide personalized and adaptive learning paths and resources.
- Sales playbook and guidance systems that use AI to provide real-time and contextual recommendations and scripts for each stage and scenario of the sales process, based on best practices, customer data, and sales performance metrics.

Customer Engagement and Experience: AI can help sales teams to deliver more personalized, proactive, and value-added customer interactions and experiences, across the entire customer lifecycle. Some examples of AI-powered customer engagement and experience tools include:

- Conversational AI platforms that use natural language processing, machine learning, and dialogue management to enable human-like conversations and interactions with customers, across multiple channels and touchpoints, and to provide personalized and contextual support, guidance, and recommendations.
- Customer intelligence and insights platforms that use AI to unify and analyze customer data from multiple sources and systems, and to provide a 360-degree view of each customer's profile, behavior, sentiment, and value, and to enable targeted and timely interventions and offers.
- Customer success and loyalty platforms that use AI to predict and prevent customer churn, to identify and promote cross-sell and upsell opportunities, and to enable proactive and personalized customer nurturing and advocacy programs.

To successfully implement and leverage AI in sales, organizations need to have a clear and compelling AI strategy and roadmap, that aligns with their sales goals, processes, and customer needs. They also need to have the right data, talent, and technology foundations in place, to enable and scale their AI initiatives and innovations. Some key considerations and best practices for implementing AI in sales include:

- Defining the business outcomes and use cases for AI in sales, and prioritizing them based on their impact, feasibility, and alignment with the sales strategy and customer experience vision.
- Assessing and improving the quality, quantity, and accessibility of sales and customer data, and establishing the data governance and management processes and tools to enable AI-driven insights and actions.
- Building and empowering a cross-functional and agile AI team, with the right mix of sales, marketing, data science, and IT skills and roles, and providing them with the resources, training, and support to drive AI innovation and adoption.
- Selecting and integrating the AI platforms and tools that best fit the sales and customer needs and processes, and that can scale and adapt as the business and market evolve, and establishing the right balance and collaboration between human and machine intelligence and decision-making.
- Measuring and optimizing the impact and ROI of AI in sales, through clear and meaningful metrics and KPIs, and through continuous testing, learning, and improvement cycles, and communicating and celebrating the successes and lessons learned with the sales team and stakeholders.

By applying AI in sales, organizations can achieve significant benefits and competitive advantages, such as:

- Improved sales productivity and efficiency, by automating

and augmenting repetitive and low-value tasks, and by providing sales reps with the right insights, content, and guidance at the right time and context.
- Increased sales effectiveness and win rates, by identifying and targeting the most promising and profitable leads and opportunities, and by delivering more personalized and value-added customer interactions and experiences.
- Enhanced sales forecasting and pipeline visibility, by leveraging predictive and prescriptive analytics to anticipate and optimize sales outcomes and risks, and to align sales plans, resources, and incentives accordingly.
- Greater sales agility and innovation, by leveraging AI to adapt and respond to changing customer needs and market dynamics, and to identify and test new sales strategies, tactics, and offerings that can drive growth and differentiation.

Some examples and case studies of successful AI applications in sales include:
- A software company that used AI-powered lead scoring and routing to increase its lead conversion rate by 30%, and to reduce its lead response time by 50%, by prioritizing and assigning leads based on their fit, intent, and behavior data, and by providing sales reps with real-time insights and recommendations on how to engage and convert them.
- A financial services firm that used AI-powered sales forecasting and pipeline management to improve its forecast accuracy by 20%, and to increase its pipeline velocity by 25%, by leveraging machine learning algorithms to predict and optimize sales outcomes and risks, and by providing sales leaders with real-time visibility and analytics on pipeline health and trends.
- A retail company that used AI-powered customer engagement and experience to increase its customer lifetime value by 15%, and to reduce its customer churn rate by 10%, by leveraging conversational AI and customer

intelligence platforms to deliver personalized and proactive customer interactions and experiences, across multiple channels and touchpoints, and to identify and act on customer needs, preferences, and behaviors in real-time.

Lessons Learned from Failed Implementations

While there are many success stories and best practices for tech-powered sales, there are also many examples and lessons learned from failed implementations and initiatives. Implementing and adopting new sales technologies and processes is not easy or straightforward, and requires careful planning, execution, and change management to avoid common pitfalls and challenges.

Here are some of the most common reasons and lessons learned from failed tech-powered sales implementations:

Lack of Clear Vision and Strategy: One of the most common reasons for failed tech-powered sales implementations is the lack of a clear and compelling vision and strategy for how the technology will support and enable the sales goals and processes. Many organizations rush to implement the latest and greatest sales technologies without first defining the business outcomes and use cases they want to achieve, and without aligning them with their sales strategy and customer needs. As a result, they end up with disconnected and underutilized technologies that don't deliver the expected value and ROI. The lesson learned is to start with the end in mind, and to define a clear and compelling vision and strategy for tech-powered sales that aligns with the sales goals, processes, and customer needs, and that provides a roadmap and prioritization for the technology investments and initiatives.

Poor Data Quality and Integration: Another common reason for failed tech-powered sales implementations is the poor quality and integration of sales and customer data across multiple systems and sources. Many organizations struggle with incomplete, inaccurate, and inconsistent data that hinders the effectiveness and adoption of sales technologies, such as CRM, sales enablement, and AI tools. They also struggle with siloed and disconnected data that prevents a holistic and real-time view of the customer and the sales process, and that requires manual and error-prone data entry and reconciliation.The lesson learned is to invest in data quality and integration as a foundation for tech-powered sales, and to establish the data governance, management, and architecture processes and tools to ensure the accuracy, completeness, and accessibility of sales and customer data across the organization.

Lack of User Adoption and Enablement: A third common reason for failed tech-powered sales implementations is the lack of user adoption and enablement of the sales technologies and processes. Many organizations underestimate the change management and training required to get sales reps and managers to embrace and utilize the new tools and workflows, and to overcome their resistance and inertia to change. They also fail to provide the right incentives, support, and resources to enable and empower the sales team to leverage the technologies for their day-to-day tasks and decisions.The lesson learned is to prioritize user adoption and enablement as a critical success factor for tech-powered sales, and to invest in the change management, communication, and training programs and tools to engage and empower the sales team to use and benefit from the technologies, and to provide ongoing feedback and improvement.

Inadequate Vendor Selection and Management: A fourth common reason for failed tech-powered sales implementations is the inadequate selection and management of the technology vendors and partners. Many organizations rush to select and implement the first or cheapest sales technology solutions they find, without thoroughly evaluating and comparing the features, capabilities, and fit with their sales needs and processes. They also fail to establish clear and measurable vendor performance and service level agreements, and to regularly monitor and manage the vendor relationships and deliverables.The lesson learned is to take a strategic and holistic approach to vendor selection and management for tech-powered sales, and to establish a rigorous and objective process for evaluating

and selecting the best-fit technology solutions and partners, based on the sales goals, processes, and customer needs, and to establish clear and mutually beneficial vendor contracts, metrics, and governance models to ensure the ongoing value and success of the implementations.

Lack of Continuous Improvement and Innovation: A fifth common reason for failed tech-powered sales implementations is the lack of continuous improvement and innovation of the sales technologies and processes. Many organizations treat the implementation of sales technologies as a one-time event or project, and fail to establish the processes and metrics to monitor, measure, and optimize the performance and impact of the technologies over time. They also fail to foster a culture of experimentation, learning, and innovation that encourages the sales team to test and adopt new tools, techniques, and best practices that can drive better results and customer experiences.The lesson learned is to embrace continuous improvement and innovation as a key principle and practice for tech-powered sales, and to establish the processes, metrics, and incentives to track, analyze, and optimize the performance and ROI of the sales technologies and processes, and to empower and reward the sales team to experiment, learn, and improve their use and impact of the technologies.

To avoid these common pitfalls and challenges, and to maximize the success and value of tech-powered sales implementations, organizations need to take a holistic and customer-centric approach that aligns the people, processes, and technologies around the sales goals and customer needs. They also need to establish strong leadership, governance, and change management practices that engage and empower the sales team and stakeholders to drive the adoption and optimization of the technologies and processes.

Some examples and case studies of failed tech-powered sales implementations include:

- A healthcare company that implemented a new CRM system without first defining the sales processes and data requirements, and without providing adequate training and support to the sales team. As a result, the CRM system was poorly adopted and utilized, with incomplete and inaccurate data, and minimal impact on sales productivity and effectiveness. The company had to restart the implementation with a more strategic and user-centric approach that aligned the CRM system with the sales goals and workflows, and that provided ongoing enablement and support to the sales team.

- A manufacturing company that selected a sales enablement platform based on the lowest price and fastest implementation, without thoroughly evaluating the features and fit with the sales content and training needs. As a result, the sales enablement platform was underutilized and disconnected from the sales process, with outdated and generic content, and limited impact on sales skills and performance. The company had to rethink its sales enablement strategy and technology, and to invest in a more comprehensive and integrated platform that aligned with the sales goals and customer needs, and that provided dynamic and personalized content and training to the sales team.

- A technology company that implemented an AI-powered sales forecasting and pipeline management tool without first establishing the data quality and governance processes, and without engaging the sales leaders and managers in the design and validation of the AI models and insights. As a result, the AI tool provided inaccurate and unreliable forecasts and recommendations, and was rejected and abandoned by the sales team, who reverted to their manual and intuitive forecasting methods. The company had to revisit its AI strategy and implementation, and to invest in data quality and integration, and in sales leadership and user involvement, to ensure the trust and adoption of the AI tool and insights.

These examples and lessons learned highlight the importance of taking a strategic, holistic, and user-centric approach to tech-powered sales implementations, and of establishing the right vision, data, people, and processes to enable and sustain the success and value of the technologies and innovations. Organizations that learn from these failures and best practices, and that continuously improve and innovate their tech-powered sales capabilities, will be better positioned to drive growth, efficiency, and customer value in the digital and data-driven world.

PART 10: ADVANCED SALES STRATEGIES

Hyper-Personalization at Scale

In today's digital and customer-centric world, personalization has become a key differentiator and driver of sales success and customer loyalty. Customers expect and demand tailored and relevant experiences and interactions that recognize their unique needs, preferences, and contexts, and that provide them with value and convenience at every touchpoint and stage of their journey.

However, delivering personalization at scale is a complex and challenging task that requires advanced data, analytics, and automation capabilities, as well as a customer-centric and agile mindset and culture. This is where hyper-personalization comes in, as a strategy and approach that leverages AI and machine learning technologies to enable real-time and dynamic personalization of sales and marketing experiences and offers, based on individual customer data and behaviors.

Hyper-personalization goes beyond traditional segmentation and targeting methods, which rely on broad and static customer attributes and rules, and instead uses advanced algorithms and models to continuously learn and adapt to each customer's evolving needs, interests, and actions, and to deliver the most relevant and engaging content, products, and services, at the right time and channel.

Here are some of the key elements and benefits of hyper-personalization at scale:

Customer Data and Insights: Hyper-personalization requires a rich and unified view of each customer, across multiple data sources and touchpoints, such as demographics, transactions, interactions, behaviors, and preferences. This data needs to be collected, integrated, and analyzed in real-time, to provide a holistic and up-to-date understanding of each customer's profile, context, and intent, and to enable targeted and timely personalization and engagement.

AI and Machine Learning: Hyper-personalization leverages AI and machine learning technologies, such as predictive analytics, recommender systems, and natural language processing, to automatically identify patterns, preferences, and opportunities in customer data, and to generate personalized and dynamic content, offers, and experiences, based on each customer's individual needs and behaviors. These technologies can also learn and optimize over time, based on customer feedback and actions, to continuously improve the relevance and effectiveness of personalization.

Omnichannel and Real-Time Engagement: Hyper-personalization enables consistent and seamless personalization across multiple channels and touchpoints, such as web, mobile, email, social, and in-store, and in real-time, based on each customer's current context and actions. This requires advanced marketing automation and customer engagement platforms, that can orchestrate and deliver personalized and coordinated experiences and messages, across the entire customer journey and lifecycle, and that can adapt and respond to customer signals and triggers in real-time.

Agile and Iterative Optimization: Hyper-personalization is not a one-time or static initiative, but a continuous and iterative process of testing, learning, and optimization, based on customer data and feedback. This requires an agile and experimentation-driven mindset and approach, that empowers sales and marketing teams to quickly design, launch, and measure personalized campaigns and experiences, and to continuously refine and improve them, based on real-time insights and results. This also requires a culture of customer-centricity and collaboration, that aligns sales, marketing, and other functions around the customer needs and journeys, and that fosters innovation and adaptation.

Some of the key benefits and outcomes of hyper-personalization at scale include:

- Increased customer engagement and loyalty, by providing relevant and valuable experiences and offers that meet each customer's individual needs and preferences, and that create emotional connections and trust.
- Improved sales and marketing efficiency and effectiveness, by targeting the right customers with the right messages and products, at the right time and channel, and by reducing waste and irrelevance in sales and marketing efforts.
- Higher conversion rates and revenues, by personalizing the sales and marketing funnel and offers, based on each customer's profile, context, and intent, and by providing tailored and compelling value propositions and incentives.
- Enhanced customer insights and innovation, by leveraging AI and machine learning to uncover new patterns, segments, and opportunities in customer data, and to enable predictive and proactive personalization and engagement.
- To successfully implement and scale hyper-personalization, organizations need to have the right data, technology, and organizational foundations and capabilities in place, including:
- A customer data platform (CDP) that can collect, integrate, and activate customer data from multiple sources and touchpoints, and provide a unified and real-time view of each customer.

- AI and machine learning platforms and tools that can analyze and predict customer behaviors and preferences, and generate personalized and dynamic content, offers, and experiences.
- Marketing automation and customer engagement platforms that can orchestrate and deliver personalized and coordinated experiences and messages, across multiple channels and touchpoints, and in real-time.
- Agile and customer-centric processes and teams that can quickly design, launch, and optimize personalized campaigns and experiences, based on customer data and feedback, and align sales, marketing, and other functions around the customer needs and journeys.
- A culture of experimentation, learning, and innovation, that empowers sales and marketing teams to test and iterate new personalization ideas and approaches, and to continuously improve and adapt to changing customer needs and behaviors.

Some examples and case studies of successful hyper-personalization at scale include:

- A retail company that used AI-powered recommender systems and customer data to personalize the product recommendations and offers for each customer, based on their browsing and purchase history, preferences, and context. This resulted in a 20% increase in conversion rates, a 15% increase in average order value, and a 10% increase in customer loyalty and retention.
- A financial services company that used machine learning and natural language processing to personalize the financial advice and services for each customer, based on their financial goals, risk profile, and life stage. This resulted in a 30% increase in customer engagement and satisfaction, a 25% increase in cross-sell and upsell revenues, and a 15% reduction in customer churn and attrition.

- A technology company that used predictive analytics and marketing automation to personalize the sales and marketing messages and experiences for each customer, based on their industry, role, and buying stage. This resulted in a 50% increase in lead generation and qualification, a 30% increase in sales pipeline and velocity, and a 20% increase in customer acquisition and lifetime value.

Orchestrating Complex Sales Campaigns

In today's complex and competitive sales landscape, orchestrating effective and impactful sales campaigns is a critical capability and differentiator for sales organizations. Sales campaigns are coordinated and targeted efforts to reach and engage specific customer segments or accounts, with the goal of generating leads, opportunities, and revenues, and building brand awareness and loyalty.

However, orchestrating complex sales campaigns is a challenging and multi-faceted task that requires advanced planning, execution, and optimization capabilities, as well as cross-functional collaboration and alignment. This is where advanced sales strategies and technologies come in, as enablers and accelerators of campaign orchestration and performance.

Here are some of the key elements and best practices of orchestrating complex sales campaigns:

Campaign Strategy and Planning: Orchestrating complex sales campaigns starts with defining a clear and compelling campaign strategy and plan, that aligns with the overall sales and business goals, and the target customer needs and behaviors. This includes identifying the campaign objectives, target audience, value proposition, messaging, tactics, channels, timeline, budget, and metrics, and creating a detailed campaign brief and roadmap that guides the execution and optimization of the campaign.

Customer Segmentation and Targeting: Orchestrating complex sales campaigns requires a deep and actionable understanding of the target customers, and a data-driven and dynamic approach to segmentation and targeting. This includes leveraging customer data and insights, such as demographics, firmographics, behaviors, and preferences, to identify and prioritize the most valuable and responsive customer segments or accounts, and to tailor the campaign messaging and tactics to their specific needs and contexts.

Content and Creative Development: Orchestrating complex sales campaigns requires a compelling and differentiated content and creative strategy, that engages and persuades the target customers, and that aligns with the campaign objectives and messaging. This includes developing a mix of content types and formats, such as emails, landing pages, videos, whitepapers, case studies, and social posts, that educate, inspire, and convert the target customers, and that reflect the brand voice and values.

Multi-Channel Execution and Coordination: Orchestrating complex sales campaigns requires a coordinated and integrated approach to multi-channel execution, that delivers a consistent and seamless customer experience across multiple touchpoints and stages of the buying journey. This includes leveraging marketing automation and customer engagement platforms, to orchestrate and deliver the campaign content and messages across channels such as email, web, social, mobile, and events, and to track and optimize the campaign performance and results.

Sales Enablement and Acceleration: Orchestrating complex sales campaigns requires a close and aligned partnership between sales and marketing, to enable and accelerate the sales process and outcomes. This includes providing sales with the right content, tools, and insights to engage and convert the target customers, and to build and advance the sales pipeline and opportunities. This also includes establishing a lead management and handoff process, that ensures a smooth and timely transition of qualified leads from marketing to sales, and that provides feedback and learning loops to optimize the campaign strategy and tactics.

Measurement and Optimization: Orchestrating complex sales campaigns requires a data-driven and agile approach to measurement and optimization, that tracks and analyzes the campaign performance and results, and that continuously improves and adapts the campaign strategy and tactics based on customer feedback and insights. This includes defining and tracking the key campaign metrics and KPIs, such as reach, engagement, conversion, pipeline, and revenue, and using marketing analytics and attribution tools to measure and optimize the campaign ROI and impact.

Some of the key benefits and outcomes of orchestrating complex sales campaigns include:

Increased sales pipeline and velocity, by generating and nurturing high-quality leads and opportunities that align with the sales goals and target customer needs and behaviors.

Improved sales and marketing alignment and efficiency, by coordinating and integrating the sales and marketing efforts and resources around the campaign objectives and customer journey, and by reducing duplication and waste in campaign execution and management.

Enhanced customer engagement and experience, by delivering a consistent and relevant campaign message and experience across multiple channels and touchpoints, and by personalizing the campaign content and offers based on customer data and insights.

Greater brand awareness and differentiation, by creating and amplifying a compelling and unique campaign story and value proposition, that resonates with the target customers and stands out from the competition.

To successfully orchestrate complex sales campaigns, organizations need to have the right strategy, skills, and systems in place, including:

A customer-centric and data-driven campaign planning and targeting approach, that aligns the campaign objectives, audience, and tactics with the sales goals and customer needs and behaviors.

A content and creative development process that produces engaging and persuasive campaign assets and messages, that reflect the brand voice and values, and that drive customer action and conversion.

A marketing automation and customer engagement platform that enables the orchestration and delivery of the campaign content and messages across multiple channels and touchpoints, and that provides real-time insights and optimization capabilities.

A sales enablement and acceleration framework that equips sales with the right content, tools, and insights to engage and convert the target customers, and that establishes a seamless lead management and handoff process between marketing and sales.

A measurement and optimization discipline that tracks and analyzes the campaign performance and results, and that continuously improves and adapts the campaign strategy and tactics based on customer feedback and insights.

Some examples and case studies of successful orchestration of complex sales campaigns include:

A technology company that orchestrated a multi-channel ABM campaign to target and engage a select group of high-value enterprise accounts, with the goal of generating new pipeline and revenue opportunities. The campaign included personalized email and direct mail, targeted digital advertising, thought leadership content, executive events, and sales enablement tools and training. The campaign resulted in a 200% increase in target account engagement, a 150% increase in pipeline value, and a 50% increase in closed-won deals, compared to the previous year.

A financial services company that orchestrated a multi-stage demand generation campaign to attract and convert new customers for its wealth management services. The campaign included educational content, webinars, calculators, and assessments, that guided prospects through the awareness, consideration, and decision stages of the buying journey, and that provided personalized recommendations and offers based on their financial goals and profile. The campaign resulted in a 300% increase in marketing qualified leads, a 50% increase in sales accepted leads, and a 25% increase in new customer acquisition, compared to the previous year.

A healthcare company that orchestrated a multi-channel patient engagement campaign to drive awareness and adoption of its new telemedicine service. The campaign included targeted email and SMS, social media, paid search, and retargeting, that promoted the benefits and ease-of-use of the service, and that provided incentives and support for patients to sign up and schedule appointments. The campaign also included a sales enablement component, that provided the sales team with scripts, objection handling, and pricing guidance, to convert the patient leads and opportunities. The campaign resulted in a 400% increase in patient registrations, a 200% increase in completed telemedicine visits, and a 90% patient satisfaction rate, within the first 6 months of launch.

Navigating Political Agendas in Large Organizations

In large and complex organizations, sales professionals often face the challenge of navigating political agendas and dynamics that can impact their ability to effectively sell and deliver value to customers. Political agendas refer to the underlying interests, motivations, and power struggles that shape the decision-making and behaviors of individuals and groups within the organization, and that can create barriers, conflicts, and opportunities for sales.

Navigating political agendas is a critical skill and strategy for sales professionals, as it enables them to understand and influence the key stakeholders and decision-makers, to build trust and credibility, and to align their sales efforts with the organizational goals and priorities. However, it is also a complex and sensitive task that requires emotional intelligence, interpersonal skills, and strategic acumen.

Here are some of the key elements and best practices of navigating political agendas in large organizations:

Stakeholder Mapping and Analysis: Navigating political agendas starts with identifying and understanding the key stakeholders and decision-makers that influence the sales process and outcomes, and their roles, relationships, interests, and influence. This includes conducting a stakeholder mapping and analysis exercise, that categorizes the stakeholders by their level of power, interest, and support, and that identifies their goals, concerns, and preferences. This also includes researching and leveraging internal and external sources, such as org charts, LinkedIn, and news, to gather intelligence and insights on the stakeholders and their political landscape.

Relationship Building and Networking: Navigating political agendas requires building and nurturing relationships and networks with the key stakeholders and influencers, both within and outside the sales function. This includes identifying and engaging the stakeholders that have the most impact and alignment with the sales goals and values, and that can serve as sponsors, champions, and connectors. This also includes investing time and effort in understanding the stakeholders' needs, challenges, and aspirations, and in providing value and support beyond the sales context, such as sharing insights, making introductions, and offering help and advice.

Communication and Influence: Navigating political agendas requires effective and persuasive communication and influence skills, that can shape the perceptions and decisions of the key stakeholders and decision-makers. This includes crafting and delivering compelling and tailored messages and stories, that articulate the value and impact of the sales efforts, and that align with the stakeholders' goals and priorities. This also includes using different influence tactics and styles, such as rational persuasion, inspirational appeal, collaboration, and consultation, depending on the stakeholder's personality, role, and context, and adapting the communication and influence approach based on the feedback and reactions.

Conflict Resolution and Negotiation: Navigating political agendas often involves dealing with conflicts, disagreements, and competing interests among the stakeholders and decision-makers, that can hinder or derail the sales process and outcomes. This includes proactively identifying and assessing the potential sources and impacts of conflicts, and developing strategies and tactics to prevent, manage, and resolve them. This also includes using effective negotiation and conflict resolution skills, such as active listening, empathy, assertiveness, and creative problem-solving, to find mutually beneficial solutions and agreements, and to build and maintain positive relationships with the stakeholders.

Alignment and Collaboration: Navigating political agendas ultimately requires aligning and collaborating with the key stakeholders and decision-makers, to drive the sales process and outcomes forward, and to create shared value and success. This includes identifying and leveraging the common goals, interests, and priorities among the stakeholders, and creating a shared vision and plan that maximizes the benefits and minimizes the risks for all parties involved. This also includes establishing clear roles, responsibilities, and accountability for the sales efforts, and fostering open communication, trust, and transparency among the stakeholders, to ensure alignment and collaboration throughout the sales cycle.

Some of the key benefits and outcomes of navigating political agendas in large organizations include:

- Increased sales effectiveness and efficiency, by understanding and influencing the key stakeholders and decision-makers that impact the sales process and outcomes, and by aligning the sales efforts with the organizational goals and priorities.
- Improved relationship and trust building, by investing time and effort in understanding and supporting the stakeholders' needs, challenges, and aspirations, and by providing value and help beyond the sales context.
- Enhanced communication and influence skills, by crafting and delivering compelling and tailored messages and stories, and by using different influence tactics and styles based on the stakeholder's personality, role, and context.
- Greater conflict resolution and negotiation abilities, by proactively identifying and managing potential sources of conflicts and disagreements, and by using effective skills and strategies to find mutually beneficial solutions and agreements.
- Stronger alignment and collaboration, by identifying and leveraging the common goals and interests among the stakeholders, and by fostering open communication, trust, and transparency throughout the sales cycle.
- To successfully navigate political agendas in large organizations, sales professionals need to have the right mindset, skills, and strategies in place, including:
- A stakeholder-centric and politically savvy approach, that prioritizes understanding and influencing the key stakeholders and decision-makers, and that aligns the sales efforts with the organizational goals and priorities.

- Strong relationship building and networking skills, that enable building and nurturing trust and credibility with the stakeholders, and that provide value and support beyond the sales context.
- Effective communication and influence abilities, that can shape the perceptions and decisions of the stakeholders, and that adapt the messaging and style based on the stakeholder's personality, role, and context.
- Conflict resolution and negotiation expertise, that can proactively identify and manage potential sources of conflicts and disagreements, and that use effective skills and strategies to find mutually beneficial solutions and agreements.
- Collaboration and alignment focus, that identifies and leverages the common goals and interests among the stakeholders, and that fosters open communication, trust, and transparency throughout the sales cycle.

Some examples and case studies of successful navigation of political agendas in large organizations include:

A sales executive at a global IT company who successfully navigated the political landscape to win a multi-million dollar deal with a large financial institution. The executive identified and mapped the key stakeholders and decision-makers across different departments and levels, including IT, finance, procurement, and legal, and tailored his messaging and value proposition to align with their specific goals and priorities. He also built strong relationships and trust with the key influencers and sponsors, by providing valuable insights and advice on industry trends and best practices, and by helping them advance their own agendas and careers. When conflicts and objections arose during the sales process, he proactively addressed and resolved them through open communication, creative problem-solving, and win-win negotiation. As a result, he secured the deal and established a long-term strategic partnership with the customer, while also earning the respect and support of the internal stakeholders and leaders.

A sales manager at a pharmaceutical company who successfully navigated the political dynamics to launch a new drug in a highly competitive and regulated market. The manager conducted a thorough stakeholder analysis and mapping, including the medical, regulatory, marketing, and sales teams, as well as the external influencers and decision-makers, such as doctors, patient advocacy groups, and payers. She then developed a comprehensive and aligned go-to-market strategy and plan, that articulated the unique value proposition and benefits of the drug, and that addressed the specific needs and concerns of each stakeholder group. She also built a cross-functional launch team and governance model, that fostered collaboration, accountability, and transparency across the different functions and levels, and that proactively identified and mitigated potential risks and issues. When resistance and pushback emerged from some stakeholders, she used her influence and negotiation skills to find common ground and create buy-in and support for the launch. As a result, she successfully launched the drug on time and on budget, exceeded the sales and market share targets, and established a strong brand and reputation in the market.

A sales director at a management consulting firm who successfully navigated the political landscape to cross-sell and upsell services to a strategic account. The director mapped and analyzed the key stakeholders and decision-makers across different business units and levels, including the C-suite, functional leaders, and project sponsors, and identified their goals, challenges, and relationships. He then developed a tailored account plan and value proposition, that showcased the firm's relevant expertise and capabilities, and that aligned with the customer's strategic priorities and initiatives. He also leveraged his internal network and relationships, to identify and engage the right subject matter experts and delivery teams, and to build credibility and trust with the customer stakeholders. When internal conflicts and resource constraints arose, he proactively communicated and negotiated with the key stakeholders, to find mutually beneficial solutions and to ensure alignment and collaboration. As a result, he expanded the account relationship and revenue by 50% year-over-year, and established the firm as a trusted advisor and partner to the customer.

PART 11: MANAGING AND SCALING SALES TEAMS

Training and Development in the Tech-Driven Era

In the tech-driven era, sales training and development has become a critical priority and differentiator for sales organizations. As sales technologies and processes continue to evolve and advance, sales professionals need to continuously learn and adapt their skills and knowledge, to stay relevant and competitive in the market. Moreover, as sales teams become more diverse and distributed, sales leaders need to provide effective and engaging training and development programs, that can scale and personalize the learning experience for each individual and role.

Sales training and development in the tech-driven era involves a holistic and strategic approach, that combines different methods, modalities, and technologies, to enable and empower sales professionals to perform at their best. It includes a range of activities and initiatives, such as onboarding, product and solution training, sales skills and methodology training, coaching and mentoring, and continuous learning and development.

Here are some of the key elements and best practices of sales training and development in the tech-driven era:

Blended Learning: Sales training and development in the tech-driven era leverages a blended learning approach, that combines different methods and modalities, such as instructor-led training (ILT), virtual instructor-led training (VILT), e-learning, mobile learning, social learning, and on-the-job learning. This approach provides flexibility, convenience, and engagement for the learners, and enables them to access and apply the learning content and activities in different ways and contexts. It also allows sales leaders to customize and optimize the learning experience, based on the learners' needs, preferences, and performance.

Microlearning: Sales training and development in the tech-driven era leverages microlearning, which involves delivering short, focused, and actionable learning content and activities, that can be easily consumed and applied by the learners. Microlearning is particularly effective for sales professionals, who have limited time and attention, and who need to quickly learn and retain critical information and skills. Microlearning can be delivered through various formats, such as videos, podcasts, infographics, quizzes, and games, and can be accessed on-demand, on any device, and in any context.

Gamification: Sales training and development in the tech-driven era leverages gamification, which involves using game design elements and mechanics, such as points, badges, leaderboards, challenges, and rewards, to engage and motivate the learners. Gamification can make the learning experience more fun, interactive, and competitive, and can increase the learners' participation, retention, and application of the learning content. Gamification can be applied to different types of learning activities, such as product knowledge quizzes, role-playing scenarios, sales simulations, and team challenges.

Personalization: Sales training and development in the tech-driven era leverages personalization, which involves tailoring the learning content, activities, and paths, to the individual learners' needs, preferences, and performance. Personalization can be achieved through various techniques, such as adaptive learning, which adjusts the learning content and difficulty based on the learners' responses and progress, and recommender systems, which suggest relevant learning content and activities based on the learners' profile and behavior. Personalization can improve the learners' engagement, motivation, and outcomes, and can enable them to learn at their own pace and style.

Collaboration: Sales training and development in the tech-driven era leverages collaboration, which involves enabling and encouraging the learners to interact, share, and learn from each other, and from subject matter experts and mentors. Collaboration can be facilitated through various tools and platforms, such as social learning networks, discussion forums, virtual classrooms, and coaching and mentoring programs. Collaboration can foster a culture of continuous learning, innovation, and best practice sharing, and can enhance the learners' skills, knowledge, and relationships.

Some of the key benefits and outcomes of effective sales training and development in the tech-driven era include:

- Increased sales productivity and performance, by equipping sales professionals with the right skills, knowledge, and tools to effectively engage and convert customers, and to achieve their sales goals and quotas.
- Improved sales onboarding and ramp-up time, by providing new sales hires with a comprehensive and engaging onboarding program, that covers the company culture, products, processes, and tools, and that accelerates their time-to-productivity and performance.
- Enhanced sales skills and methodology adoption, by providing sales professionals with a consistent and proven sales methodology and framework, that guides their sales activities and conversations, and that improves their effectiveness and efficiency.

- Greater sales coaching and mentoring impact, by providing sales managers and leaders with the skills, tools, and processes to effectively coach and mentor their teams, and to drive their performance and development.
- Stronger sales culture and engagement, by fostering a culture of continuous learning, collaboration, and innovation, and by engaging and motivating sales professionals to learn, grow, and succeed in their roles and careers.
- To successfully implement and scale sales training and development in the tech-driven era, sales organizations need to have the right strategy, infrastructure, and governance in place, including:
- A sales training and development strategy and roadmap, that aligns with the overall sales strategy and goals, and that defines the learning objectives, audiences, modalities, and metrics for each program and initiative.
- A sales training and development infrastructure and technology stack, that includes a learning management system (LMS), content authoring and delivery tools, social and collaborative learning platforms, and analytics and reporting capabilities.
- A sales training and development governance and operating model, that defines the roles, responsibilities, and processes for designing, developing, delivering, and evaluating the learning programs and initiatives, and that ensures alignment and collaboration with the sales, marketing, product, and HR functions.
- A sales training and development measurement and optimization framework, that tracks and analyzes the learning engagement, performance, and impact metrics, and that continuously improves and innovates the learning programs and initiatives based on the feedback and results.

Some examples and case studies of successful sales training and development programs in the tech-driven era include:

A global IT company that implemented a blended and personalized sales onboarding program, that combined instructor-led training, e-learning, mobile learning, and on-the-job learning, and that tailored the learning paths and content to the different sales roles and regions. The program also leveraged gamification and social learning, to engage and motivate the new hires, and to foster collaboration and best practice sharing. As a result, the company reduced the sales onboarding time by 50%, increased the new hire retention rate by 25%, and improved the sales productivity and quota attainment by 30%.

A financial services company that implemented a microlearning and adaptive learning program, to upskill and reskill its sales professionals on the new products, regulations, and customer needs. The program delivered short and focused learning modules and quizzes, that adapted to the learners' knowledge and performance, and that provided personalized feedback and recommendations. The program also leveraged mobile learning and gamification, to enable the learners to access and apply the learning content anytime and anywhere, and to compete and collaborate with their peers. As a result, the company increased the product knowledge and sales readiness by 40%, improved the customer satisfaction and loyalty by 20%, and increased the cross-sell and upsell revenue by 15%.

A pharmaceutical company that implemented a virtual and collaborative sales coaching program, to enable its sales managers to effectively coach and develop their remote and distributed teams. The program provided the sales managers with a virtual coaching platform and toolkit, that included video conferencing, call recording and analysis, performance dashboards, and coaching templates and guides. The program also leveraged social learning and gamification, to enable the sales managers to share and recognize best practices and successes, and to motivate and engage their teams. As a result, the company increased the sales coaching frequency and quality by 50%, improved the sales rep engagement and retention by 30%, and increased the sales pipeline and win rate by 25%.

Performance Metrics and KPIs

Sales performance metrics and key performance indicators (KPIs) are critical tools and frameworks for managing and scaling sales teams effectively. They provide a clear and objective way to measure and track the sales team's progress and success, against the defined goals and targets. They also enable sales leaders to identify the strengths, weaknesses, and opportunities for improvement, and to make data-driven decisions and actions to optimize the sales team's performance and results.

Sales performance metrics and KPIs can vary depending on the company's industry, market, product, and growth stage, as well as the sales team's structure, roles, and responsibilities. However, there are some common and essential metrics and KPIs that most sales organizations use to manage and scale their teams, such as:

Sales Revenue: This is the most fundamental and important metric for sales teams, as it measures the total amount of revenue generated from sales activities, over a given period of time. Sales revenue can be broken down by different dimensions, such as product line, customer segment, sales channel, and sales rep, to provide more granular and actionable insights. Sales revenue growth and attainment against the target are key indicators of the sales team's performance and impact on the business.

Sales Quota Attainment: This metric measures the percentage of sales reps who meet or exceed their assigned sales quota, over a given period of time. Sales quota is the target revenue or units that each sales rep is expected to achieve, based on their role, territory, and market potential. Sales quota attainment is a key indicator of the sales team's productivity, effectiveness, and motivation, and can help identify the top performers and the areas for coaching and development.

Sales Pipeline: This metric measures the total value and volume of the sales opportunities that are in the different stages of the sales process, from prospecting to closing. Sales pipeline provides a forward-looking view of the sales team's potential revenue and growth, and can help forecast and manage the sales resources and activities. Key sales pipeline metrics include pipeline value, pipeline velocity, pipeline conversion rate, and pipeline coverage ratio, which measures the ratio of the pipeline value to the sales quota.

Sales Cycle Length: This metric measures the average time it takes for a sales opportunity to move from the initial contact to the closed deal, over a given period of time. Sales cycle length can vary depending on the complexity and value of the product or service, the decision-making process and stakeholders involved, and the sales team's skills and approach. Reducing the sales cycle length can help accelerate the revenue growth and improve the sales team's efficiency and productivity.

Win Rate: This metric measures the percentage of sales opportunities that are successfully closed as won deals, over a given period of time. Win rate is a key indicator of the sales team's effectiveness and competitiveness, and can help identify the best practices and areas for improvement in the sales process and approach. Win rate can be measured at different levels, such as by sales rep, product line, customer segment, and sales stage, to provide more actionable insights.

Customer Acquisition Cost (CAC): This metric measures the total cost of acquiring a new customer, including the sales and marketing expenses, over a given period of time. CAC is a key indicator of the sales team's efficiency and profitability, and can help optimize the sales investments and resources. CAC can be compared to the customer lifetime value (LTV), which measures the total revenue generated from a customer over their lifetime, to assess the sales team's return on investment (ROI) and long-term growth potential.

Customer Retention and Expansion: These metrics measure the sales team's ability to retain and grow the existing customer relationships, over a given period of time. Customer retention rate measures the percentage of customers who continue to buy or renew their contracts, while customer expansion rate measures the percentage of customers who buy additional products or services, or increase their contract value. These metrics are key indicators of the sales team's customer satisfaction, loyalty, and upselling/cross-selling effectiveness, and can help drive the long-term revenue growth and profitability.

To effectively define, track, and use sales performance metrics and KPIs, sales organizations need to have the right data, tools, and processes in place, including:

- A clear and aligned sales strategy and goals, that define the target markets, customers, products, and growth objectives, and that cascade down to the sales team's roles, responsibilities, and quotas.
- A robust and integrated sales technology stack, that includes a customer relationship management (CRM) system, sales enablement and coaching tools, and analytics and reporting capabilities, to capture, manage, and analyze the sales data and activities.
- A consistent and standardized sales process and methodology, that defines the key stages, activities, and milestones of the sales cycle, and that enables the sales team to effectively qualify, advance, and close the sales opportunities.
- A regular and actionable sales performance review and feedback cadence, that involves the sales leaders, managers, and reps, and that uses the metrics and KPIs to assess the progress, identify the gaps and opportunities, and define the improvement actions and plans.

- A continuous learning and development mindset and culture, that supports and encourages the sales team to learn from the metrics and KPIs, to experiment and innovate with new approaches and best practices, and to share and collaborate with each other.

Some best practices and tips for managing and scaling sales teams with performance metrics and KPIs include:

- Focus on the few key metrics that matter most for the sales team's success and growth, and align them with the company's overall goals and priorities.
- Set realistic and achievable targets for the metrics and KPIs, based on the market potential, sales capacity, and historical performance, and adjust them regularly based on the changing conditions and feedback.
- Provide clear and timely visibility and communication of the metrics and KPIs to the sales team, and enable them to easily access and analyze their own performance data and trends.
- Use the metrics and KPIs to identify the top performers and best practices, and to recognize and reward them for their achievements and contributions.
- Use the metrics and KPIs to identify the underperformers and areas for improvement, and to provide targeted coaching, training, and support to help them improve and succeed.
- Use the metrics and KPIs to inform and optimize the sales planning, forecasting, and resource allocation decisions, and to adapt and innovate the sales strategies and tactics based on the changing market and customer needs.
- Use the metrics and KPIs to benchmark and compare the sales team's performance against the industry peers and best practices, and to identify the areas for differentiation and competitive advantage.

Some examples and case studies of successful use of sales

performance metrics and KPIs include:

A software company that implemented a data-driven sales performance management system, that tracked and analyzed the key metrics such as sales revenue, quota attainment, pipeline velocity, and win rate, across the different sales roles, regions, and products. The system provided real-time and actionable insights and alerts to the sales leaders and managers, and enabled them to proactively identify and address the performance gaps and opportunities. As a result, the company increased the sales productivity by 20%, the pipeline conversion rate by 15%, and the revenue growth by 25% year-over-year.

A manufacturing company that used the customer acquisition cost (CAC) and customer lifetime value (LTV) metrics to optimize its sales investments and resources across the different customer segments and channels. The company segmented its customers based on their profitability and growth potential, and allocated the sales budgets and headcounts based on the CAC/LTV ratios and ROI. The company also used the metrics to identify the most effective and efficient sales channels and tactics for each segment, and to continuously test and optimize them based on the results. As a result, the company reduced the CAC by 30%, increased the LTV by 20%, and improved the sales ROI by 50%.

A professional services firm that used the sales cycle length and win rate metrics to improve its sales process and methodology, and to accelerate its revenue growth and market share. The firm analyzed the sales cycle length and win rate data across the different sales stages, deal sizes, and client industries, and identified the key bottlenecks, best practices, and improvement opportunities. The firm then redesigned its sales process and methodology based on the insights, and provided targeted training and coaching to the sales team to adopt and apply the new approach. As a result, the firm reduced the average sales cycle length by 25%, increased the win rate by 20%, and grew its revenue and market share by 30% in the first year of implementation.

Building a Resilient Sales Culture

A resilient sales culture is one that can adapt, bounce back, and thrive in the face of challenges, changes, and uncertainties. It is a culture that fosters the mindsets, behaviors, and processes that enable the sales team to continuously learn, grow, and succeed, despite the external and internal pressures and obstacles. Building a resilient sales culture is critical for managing and scaling sales teams effectively, as it can help improve the sales team's engagement, performance, and retention, and drive the long-term and sustainable growth and competitiveness of the organization.

Here are some of the key elements and best practices of building a resilient sales culture:

Purpose and Values: A resilient sales culture starts with a clear and compelling purpose and set of values that guide and inspire the sales team's actions and decisions. The purpose defines the sales team's reason for being and the impact it wants to create for the customers, the company, and the society. The values define the sales team's core beliefs and principles that shape its behaviors and relationships. A strong and aligned purpose and values can help the sales team navigate the challenges and changes, make tough decisions, and stay motivated and committed to its goals.

Leadership and Communication: A resilient sales culture requires strong and effective leadership and communication at all levels of the sales organization. The sales leaders need to set the tone, direction, and expectations for the sales team, and to role model the resilient mindsets and behaviors. They also need to communicate openly, transparently, and frequently with the sales team, to keep them informed, engaged, and aligned with the sales strategy and goals. The sales managers need to provide ongoing coaching, feedback, and support to the sales reps, to help them develop the skills, confidence, and resilience to succeed in their roles.

Learning and Development: A resilient sales culture prioritizes continuous learning and development as a key driver of the sales team's growth and success. The sales organization needs to provide the sales team with the resources, opportunities, and incentives to learn and develop their skills, knowledge, and capabilities, both formally and informally. This can include training programs, coaching sessions, mentoring relationships, peer learning groups, and self-directed learning resources. The sales team also needs to have a growth mindset and a willingness to experiment, take risks, and learn from failures and successes, in order to adapt and improve their performance over time.

Collaboration and Teamwork: A resilient sales culture fosters strong collaboration and teamwork among the sales team members, as well as with other functions and stakeholders. The sales team needs to work together effectively to share information, ideas, and best practices, to solve problems and challenges, and to support and motivate each other. The sales organization needs to promote a culture of trust, respect, and inclusion, where diverse perspectives and contributions are valued and leveraged. The sales team also needs to collaborate closely with other functions, such as marketing, product, and customer success, to align and integrate their efforts and to deliver a seamless and value-added customer experience.

Recognition and Rewards: A resilient sales culture recognizes and rewards the sales team's achievements, efforts, and contributions, both individually and collectively. The sales organization needs to have a fair and transparent system for setting goals, measuring performance, and providing feedback and incentives to the sales team. The recognition and rewards should be aligned with the sales team's purpose and values, and should reinforce the behaviors and outcomes that drive the sales team's success and growth. The recognition and rewards should also be meaningful, timely, and personalized to the individual sales team members, based on their unique strengths, interests, and motivations.

To build a resilient sales culture, sales organizations need to take a holistic and intentional approach that involves the following steps:

Assess the current sales culture: Conduct a thorough assessment of the current sales culture, using surveys, interviews, focus groups, and observations, to identify the strengths, weaknesses, and opportunities for improvement. Involve the sales team members and other stakeholders in the assessment, to gather their perspectives and insights.

Define the desired sales culture: Based on the assessment results and the sales strategy and goals, define the desired sales culture that aligns with the organization's purpose and values, and that enables the sales team to thrive and succeed in the long term. Articulate the key mindsets, behaviors, and processes that characterize the desired sales culture, and communicate them clearly and consistently to the sales team and other stakeholders.

Develop a culture change plan: Develop a comprehensive and actionable plan to transform the current sales culture into the desired one, using a range of interventions and initiatives, such as leadership development, communication campaigns, training programs, recognition and rewards systems, and performance management processes. Prioritize and sequence the initiatives based on their impact, feasibility, and alignment with the sales strategy and goals.

Engage and empower the sales team: Engage and empower the sales team members to co-create and co-own the sales culture change process, by involving them in the planning, implementation, and evaluation of the initiatives. Provide them with the resources, support, and autonomy to experiment, learn, and adapt their mindsets and behaviors, and to share their feedback and ideas for improvement.

Monitor and measure the progress: Monitor and measure the progress and impact of the sales culture change initiatives, using a range of metrics and indicators, such as employee engagement, customer satisfaction, sales performance, and retention rates. Celebrate the successes and milestones, and adjust the initiatives based on the feedback and results, to ensure continuous improvement and sustainability of the sales culture change.

Some examples and case studies of successful building of resilient sales cultures include:

A technology company that transformed its sales culture from a transactional and short-term focused one to a collaborative and customer-centric one, by redefining its sales purpose and values, and aligning its sales processes, metrics, and incentives with them. The company also invested in leadership development, communication, and training programs to equip the sales team with the mindsets and skills to build long-term and value-added customer relationships. As a result, the company increased its customer retention rate by 30%, its sales team engagement score by 20%, and its revenue growth by 15% year-over-year.

A financial services firm that built a resilient sales culture that prioritized learning, experimentation, and innovation, by providing its sales team with the resources, opportunities, and incentives to continuously develop their skills and knowledge, and to test and implement new ideas and approaches. The firm also fostered a culture of psychological safety, where the sales team felt comfortable taking risks, making mistakes, and learning from them. As a result, the firm increased its sales team's adaptability and agility, as well as its ability to respond to changing customer needs and market conditions, leading to a 25% increase in sales productivity and a 20% reduction in turnover rate.

A healthcare company that strengthened its sales culture's collaboration and teamwork, by breaking down the silos and barriers between the sales team and other functions, such as marketing, product, and customer success. The company implemented cross-functional teams, projects, and meetings to align and integrate the efforts and expertise of different functions, and to deliver a seamless and value-added customer experience. The company also recognized and rewarded the sales team's collaboration and contribution to the overall organizational goals and success. As a result, the company increased its sales team's engagement and satisfaction, as well as its ability to cross-sell and upsell to existing customers, leading to a 30% increase in customer lifetime value and a 20% increase in market share.

PART 12: FUTURE TRENDS IN SALES

Predicting the Next Decade in Sales Technology

The sales technology landscape is rapidly evolving and transforming, driven by the advances in artificial intelligence, machine learning, big data, and cloud computing, as well as the changing customer expectations and behaviors. In the next decade, we can expect to see a range of new and disruptive sales technologies that will fundamentally change the way sales teams work, interact with customers, and drive business growth and competitiveness.

Here are some of the key trends and predictions for the next decade in sales technology:

Conversational AI and Chatbots: Conversational AI and chatbots will become increasingly prevalent and sophisticated in sales, enabling sales teams to automate and personalize the customer interactions and support across multiple channels, such as website, mobile, social media, and messaging platforms. Conversational AI will use natural language processing, machine learning, and sentiment analysis to understand and respond to customer queries, needs, and emotions, and to provide relevant and timely information, recommendations, and solutions. Chatbots will also be integrated with sales enablement and CRM systems, to provide sales reps with real-time customer insights, guidance, and automation of routine tasks and processes.

Augmented and Virtual Reality: Augmented reality (AR) and virtual reality (VR) will become more mainstream and impactful in sales, enabling sales teams to create immersive and interactive customer experiences that showcase products, solutions, and value propositions in new and compelling ways. AR will allow sales reps to overlay digital information and simulations onto the physical world, such as product demos, user guides, and customer testimonials, using mobile devices and smart glasses. VR will allow sales reps to create fully immersive and customizable environments, such as virtual showrooms, training simulations, and customer co-creation sessions, using headsets and controllers.

Predictive and Prescriptive Analytics: Predictive and prescriptive analytics will become more advanced and actionable in sales, enabling sales teams to anticipate and optimize the customer needs, behaviors, and outcomes, and to make data-driven decisions and actions. Predictive analytics will use machine learning algorithms and models to analyze large and diverse datasets, such as customer demographics, transactions, interactions, and feedback, to predict the likelihood and value of future customer actions, such as purchases, churn, and referrals. Prescriptive analytics will use optimization and simulation techniques to recommend the best course of action for sales reps, such as the most effective sales tactics, offers, and pricing for each customer segment and stage of the buying journey.

Sales Automation and AI Assistants: Sales automation and AI assistants will become more integrated and intelligent in sales, enabling sales teams to streamline and optimize the end-to-end sales process and experience. Sales automation will use robotic process automation (RPA) and machine learning to automate and standardize the repetitive and manual sales tasks and workflows, such as lead generation, qualification, and follow-up, freeing up sales reps to focus on more strategic and value-added activities. AI assistants will use natural language processing and generation to provide sales reps with real-time and personalized guidance, recommendations, and insights, based on the customer data, sales playbooks, and best practices, and to assist with the sales conversations, presentations, and negotiations.

Blockchain and Smart Contracts: Blockchain and smart contracts will become more relevant and transformative in sales, enabling sales teams to create secure, transparent, and automated sales transactions and agreements with customers and partners. Blockchain will use distributed ledger technology to record and verify the sales data and documents, such as customer identities, orders, invoices, and payments, in a tamper-proof and auditable manner, reducing the risk of fraud, errors, and disputes. Smart contracts will use self-executing and self-enforcing code to automate the terms and conditions of sales contracts, such as pricing, discounts, delivery, and warranties, based on predefined rules and triggers, reducing the time and cost of contract management and compliance.

To prepare for and leverage these future trends and technologies in sales, organizations need to take a proactive and strategic approach that involves the following steps:

Monitor and assess the trends and technologies: Continuously monitor and assess the emerging trends and technologies in sales, using a range of sources and frameworks, such as industry reports, analyst firms, technology vendors, and customer feedback. Evaluate the potential impact, benefits, and risks of each trend and technology on the sales strategy, process, and performance, and prioritize them based on their alignment with the organizational goals and capabilities.

Develop a sales technology roadmap and strategy: Based on the assessment and prioritization, develop a clear and actionable sales technology roadmap and strategy that outlines the short-term and long-term initiatives and investments needed to adopt and integrate the relevant trends and technologies into the sales organization. Define the key objectives, milestones, and metrics for each initiative, and align them with the overall sales and business strategy and goals.

Build the sales technology capabilities and ecosystem: Build the necessary sales technology capabilities and ecosystem to support and enable the adoption and scaling of the trends and technologies. This includes developing the sales technology skills and talent, both internally and externally, through training, hiring, and partnering with technology providers and experts. It also includes establishing the sales technology infrastructure and architecture, such as data platforms, integration layers, and security frameworks, to ensure the interoperability, scalability, and reliability of the sales technology stack.

Pilot and scale the sales technology initiatives: Pilot and scale the sales technology initiatives in a phased and iterative manner, starting with small and low-risk experiments and use cases, and gradually expanding and optimizing them based on the results and learnings. Involve the sales team members and other stakeholders in the design, testing, and evaluation of the initiatives, to gather their feedback and buy-in, and to ensure the usability and value of the sales technologies. Measure and communicate the impact and ROI of the initiatives, using a range of quantitative and qualitative metrics, such as sales productivity, customer satisfaction, and innovation rate.

Foster a sales technology culture and mindset: Foster a sales technology culture and mindset that embraces and promotes the continuous learning, experimentation, and innovation with the trends and technologies. Encourage and incentivize the sales team members to explore and adopt new sales technologies and approaches, and to share their insights and best practices with each other and with other functions. Cultivate a data-driven and customer-centric mindset that leverages the sales technologies to generate and act on the customer insights and feedback, and to deliver personalized and value-added sales experiences.

Some examples and case studies of successful adoption and leveraging of future sales technologies include:

A retail company that implemented a conversational AI and chatbot platform to provide 24/7 customer support and personalized product recommendations across its website, mobile app, and social media channels. The chatbot used natural language processing and machine learning to understand and respond to customer queries and preferences, and to provide relevant and timely information and offers. As a result, the company increased its online conversion rate by 30%, reduced its customer support costs by 25%, and improved its customer satisfaction score by 20%.

A manufacturing company that used augmented reality and virtual reality to create immersive and interactive product demos and training simulations for its sales team and customers. The AR and VR experiences allowed the sales reps to showcase the features and benefits of the complex and customizable products in a more engaging and memorable way, and to provide the customers with hands-on and realistic product trials and configurations. As a result, the company increased its sales cycle speed by 20%, its deal size by 15%, and its customer retention rate by 10%.

A financial services firm that leveraged predictive and prescriptive analytics to optimize its sales coverage and resource allocation across different customer segments and territories. The analytics models used machine learning algorithms to analyze the customer data, such as demographics, transactions, and interactions, and to predict the customer lifetime value, churn risk, and cross-sell potential. The models also provided the sales reps with real-time and actionable recommendations on the best sales tactics, offers, and pricing for each customer based on their profile and behavior. As a result, the firm increased its sales revenue by 25%, its sales productivity by 20%, and its customer acquisition cost by 15%.

The Role of Big Data and Analytics

Big data and analytics are playing an increasingly critical and transformative role in sales, enabling sales organizations to gain deeper and more actionable insights into customer needs, behaviors, and outcomes, and to make data-driven decisions and actions that improve sales performance and competitiveness. Big data refers to the large and diverse volumes of structured and unstructured data generated by customers, products, and processes, such as transactions, interactions, social media, and sensor data. Analytics refers to the techniques and tools used to collect, process, analyze, and visualize the big data, such as statistical modeling, machine learning, and data visualization.

Here are some of the key ways in which big data and analytics are impacting and advancing sales:

Customer Segmentation and Targeting: Big data and analytics enable sales organizations to create more granular and dynamic customer segmentation and targeting models, based on a wide range of customer attributes and behaviors, such as demographics, psychographics, purchase history, channel preferences, and social media activity. These models help sales teams to identify and prioritize the most valuable and profitable customer segments, and to tailor their sales strategies, tactics, and offers to the specific needs and preferences of each segment. For example, a retail company can use big data and analytics to segment its customers based on their shopping frequency, basket size, and product categories, and to target them with personalized promotions, recommendations, and loyalty programs.

Sales Forecasting and Planning: Big data and analytics enable sales organizations to create more accurate and timely sales forecasting and planning models, based on a wide range of internal and external data sources, such as sales pipeline, market trends, economic indicators, and competitor activity. These models help sales teams to predict and plan their sales revenue, margin, and growth, and to allocate their sales resources and budgets accordingly. For example, a software company can use big data and analytics to forecast its sales pipeline and revenue, based on factors such as lead volume, conversion rates, deal size, and sales cycle length, and to adjust its sales headcount, territories, and quotas based on the forecast.

Sales Performance Management: Big data and analytics enable sales organizations to create more comprehensive and actionable sales performance management frameworks, based on a wide range of sales metrics and key performance indicators (KPIs), such as sales revenue, quota attainment, win rate, sales cycle time, and customer satisfaction. These frameworks help sales teams to measure, monitor, and optimize their sales performance, and to identify the drivers and barriers of sales success. For example, a financial services firm can use big data and analytics to track and analyze the sales performance of its sales reps and managers, across different products, regions, and customer segments, and to provide them with real-time feedback, coaching, and incentives based on their performance.

Customer Engagement and Experience: Big data and analytics enable sales organizations to create more personalized and seamless customer engagement and experience strategies, based on a wide range of customer touchpoints and interactions, such as website, mobile, email, social media, and in-person. These strategies help sales teams to understand and anticipate customer needs, preferences, and behaviors, and to deliver relevant and timely information, recommendations, and solutions across the customer journey. For example, a healthcare company can use big data and analytics to analyze the customer interactions and feedback across multiple channels, and to provide its sales reps with real-time guidance and content to engage and support the customers at each stage of the buying process.

Sales Enablement and Training: Big data and analytics enable sales organizations to create more effective and scalable sales enablement and training programs, based on a wide range of sales skills, knowledge, and best practices. These programs help sales teams to develop and apply the competencies and behaviors that drive sales success, and to continuously learn and improve their performance. For example, a manufacturing company can use big data and analytics to analyze the sales conversations, presentations, and proposals of its top-performing sales reps, and to identify the key skills, messages, and techniques that contribute to their success. The company can then use these insights to create and deliver targeted sales enablement and training content and activities, such as playbooks, simulations, and coaching sessions, to help other sales reps to adopt and apply the best practices.

To effectively leverage big data and analytics in sales, organizations need to have the right data, technology, and talent foundations and capabilities in place, including:

Data Strategy and Governance: A clear and aligned data strategy and governance framework that defines the data vision, goals, policies, and standards for the sales organization, and that ensures the quality, security, privacy, and compliance of the sales data across the data lifecycle.

Data Infrastructure and Architecture: A robust and scalable data infrastructure and architecture that enables the collection, storage, processing, and analysis of the sales data, using technologies such as data warehouses, data lakes, cloud platforms, and big data tools.

Data Integration and Management: A comprehensive and automated data integration and management process that enables the extraction, transformation, loading, and synchronization of the sales data from multiple sources and systems, such as CRM, marketing automation, customer service, and social media, and that ensures the consistency, accuracy, and timeliness of the data.

Analytics and Visualization Tools: A set of advanced and user-friendly analytics and visualization tools that enable the exploration, modeling, and communication of the sales data and insights, using techniques such as data mining, predictive modeling, machine learning, and data visualization, and that provide the sales teams with actionable and impactful information and recommendations.

Data Science and Analytics Talent: A team of skilled and experienced data scientists, analysts, and engineers that can design, develop, and deploy the big data and analytics solutions for sales, and that can collaborate with the sales teams and other stakeholders to translate the data insights into business value and impact.

Some examples and case studies of successful leveraging of big data and analytics in sales include:

A consumer goods company that used big data and analytics to optimize its sales territory and route planning, based on factors such as store density, traffic patterns, and sales potential. The company analyzed the geospatial and transactional data of its stores and customers, and used machine learning algorithms to cluster and prioritize the stores and routes based on their similarity and proximity. As a result, the company increased its sales coverage and efficiency by 20%, reduced its sales travel time and cost by 15%, and improved its store service level and customer satisfaction by 10%.

A technology company that used big data and analytics to improve its sales lead generation and qualification process, based on factors such as lead source, behavior, and profile. The company analyzed the web, email, and social media data of its leads, and used predictive modeling to score and rank the leads based on their likelihood to convert and their potential value. The company also used natural language processing to analyze the lead interactions and feedback, and to provide the sales reps with personalized talking points and content. As a result, the company increased its lead conversion rate by 30%, reduced its lead response time by 25%, and improved its sales pipeline quality and velocity by 20%.

A professional services firm that used big data and analytics to enhance its sales talent acquisition and development programs, based on factors such as sales competencies, performance, and potential. The company analyzed the sales activity, outcome, and feedback data of its sales reps and managers, and used machine learning to identify the key skills, behaviors, and experiences that predict sales success. The company also used data visualization to create interactive and personalized sales talent dashboards and reports, that provide the sales leaders with insights and recommendations on how to attract, develop, and retain top sales talent. As a result, the company increased its sales talent quality and diversity by 25%, reduced its sales talent turnover by 20%, and improved its sales talent engagement and productivity by 15%.

Preparing for the Future of Sales Jobs

The future of sales jobs is rapidly evolving and transforming, driven by the advances in technology, the changes in customer expectations and behaviors, and the shifts in business models and strategies. In the next decade and beyond, we can expect to see a range of new and emerging sales roles, skills, and career paths, that will require sales professionals to continuously learn, adapt, and innovate to stay relevant and competitive.

Here are some of the key trends and predictions for the future of sales jobs:

Sales Enablement and Operations: Sales enablement and operations roles will become increasingly important and strategic, as sales organizations focus on optimizing the end-to-end sales process and experience, and on providing the sales teams with the right tools, content, and support to drive sales performance and growth. Sales enablement and operations professionals will be responsible for designing, implementing, and managing the sales enablement and operations programs and platforms, such as sales training, coaching, content management, and analytics, and for collaborating with other functions, such as marketing, product, and customer success, to align and integrate the sales efforts.

Sales Technology and Analytics: Sales technology and analytics roles will become increasingly prevalent and specialized, as sales organizations leverage advanced technologies, such as artificial intelligence, machine learning, and big data, to gain insights, automate tasks, and enhance decision-making. Sales technology and analytics professionals will be responsible for designing, developing, and deploying the sales technology and analytics solutions, such as CRM, sales automation, predictive modeling, and data visualization, and for partnering with the sales teams and other stakeholders to translate the technology and data into business value and impact.

Sales Consulting and Advisory: Sales consulting and advisory roles will become increasingly valued and sought-after, as sales organizations focus on providing strategic and value-added services to customers, and on building long-term and trusted relationships. Sales consulting and advisory professionals will be responsible for understanding the customer's business challenges and opportunities, and for providing them with insights, recommendations, and solutions that address their specific needs and goals. They will also be responsible for managing the customer relationships and accounts, and for identifying and pursuing new revenue streams and growth opportunities.

Sales Innovation and Transformation: Sales innovation and transformation roles will become increasingly critical and influential, as sales organizations face disruption and change, and as they seek to adapt and differentiate their sales strategies and models. Sales innovation and transformation professionals will be responsible for leading and driving the sales innovation and transformation initiatives, such as new sales channels, pricing models, and customer experiences, and for fostering a culture of experimentation, learning, and agility in the sales organization.

Sales Leadership and Coaching: Sales leadership and coaching roles will become increasingly important and challenging, as sales organizations face complex and dynamic environments, and as they seek to attract, develop, and retain top sales talent. Sales leaders and coaches will be responsible for setting the vision, strategy, and goals for the sales organization, and for inspiring, motivating, and empowering the sales teams to achieve them. They will also be responsible for providing the sales teams with ongoing feedback, guidance, and development opportunities, and for creating a positive and inclusive sales culture and environment.

To prepare for and succeed in the future of sales jobs, sales professionals need to develop and demonstrate a range of key skills and competencies, including:

Customer-Centricity and Empathy: The ability to understand and empathize with the customer's needs, challenges, and goals, and to provide them with personalized and value-added solutions and experiences.

Business Acumen and Strategic Thinking: The ability to understand and analyze the business and market trends, drivers, and opportunities, and to develop and execute sales strategies and plans that align with the organizational goals and priorities.

Technology and Data Literacy: The ability to understand and leverage the sales technologies and data, and to use them to gain insights, automate tasks, and enhance decision-making and performance.

Collaboration and Influence: The ability to collaborate and communicate effectively with cross-functional teams and stakeholders, and to influence and persuade them to support and adopt the sales initiatives and solutions.

Continuous Learning and Adaptability: The ability to continuously learn and adapt to new sales skills, technologies, and approaches, and to embrace change and uncertainty as opportunities for growth and innovation.

To attract, develop, and retain the future sales talent, organizations need to create and offer compelling and differentiated sales career paths and experiences, that provide the sales professionals with:

Meaningful and Impactful Work: The opportunity to work on sales projects and initiatives that have a significant and positive impact on the customers, the organization, and the society, and that align with their personal values and interests.

Learning and Development Opportunities: The access to ongoing and relevant sales training, coaching, and mentoring programs, that help them to develop and apply the skills and competencies needed for the future sales roles and challenges.

Technology and Data Enablement: The provision of advanced and user-friendly sales technologies and data platforms, that enable them to work more efficiently, effectively, and intelligently, and to focus on high-value and strategic activities.

Collaborative and Inclusive Culture: The creation of a sales culture and environment that promotes diversity, equity, and inclusion, and that fosters collaboration, innovation, and well-being among the sales teams and stakeholders.

Competitive and Fair Compensation: The offering of competitive and fair compensation and benefits packages, that recognize and reward the sales professionals for their performance, potential, and contributions, and that provide them with financial security and growth opportunities.

Some examples and case studies of successful preparation and development of future sales talent include:

A global technology company that created a sales academy program to attract, develop, and retain early-career sales talent from diverse backgrounds. The program provides the sales trainees with a 6-month immersive and experiential learning journey, that combines classroom training, on-the-job learning, mentoring, and coaching, and that covers a range of sales skills, such as product knowledge, customer discovery , objection handling, and negotiation. The program also provides the sales trainees with exposure and access to senior sales leaders and customers, and with opportunities to work on real sales projects and challenges. As a result, the company has increased its sales talent diversity and inclusion by 30%, improved its sales talent retention and engagement by 25%, and accelerated its sales talent time-to-productivity and performance by 20%.

A financial services firm that created a sales innovation lab to foster and support the development and implementation of new sales ideas, technologies, and models. The lab provides a safe and collaborative space for sales professionals, managers, and leaders to experiment, test, and scale sales innovations, such as new sales channels, pricing models, and customer experiences. The lab also provides the sales innovators with access to resources, expertise, and funding, and with recognition and rewards for their contributions and impact. As a result, the firm has increased its sales innovation pipeline and velocity by 50%, improved its sales innovation success rate and ROI by 30%, and enhanced its sales innovation culture and reputation by 25%.

A healthcare company that created a sales coaching and mentoring program to support the continuous learning and development of its sales teams and leaders. The program provides the sales professionals with access to a network of internal and external sales coaches and mentors, who provide them with ongoing feedback, guidance, and support on their sales skills, performance, and career goals. The program also provides the sales coaches and mentors with training, tools, and recognition for their roles and contributions. As a result, the company has increased its sales coaching and mentoring engagement and satisfaction by 40%, improved its sales coaching and mentoring effectiveness and impact by 30%, and enhanced its sales coaching and mentoring brand and talent attraction by 25%.

PART 13: TOOLS AND RESOURCES

Recommended Sales Tech Tools

Sales technology tools have become essential for modern sales organizations to improve efficiency, effectiveness, and customer experience. With the rapid advancement of technology, there is a wide range of sales tech tools available in the market, catering to different sales processes, roles, and requirements. Here are some of the recommended sales tech tools for organizations to consider:

Customer Relationship Management (CRM) Systems:

Salesforce: A cloud-based CRM platform that provides a comprehensive set of tools for sales, customer service, marketing, and analytics.

HubSpot CRM: A free and user-friendly CRM system that offers contact management, deal tracking, and email integration.

Microsoft Dynamics 365: A flexible and scalable CRM solution that integrates with other Microsoft tools and provides AI-powered insights.

Sales Engagement Platforms:

Outreach: A sales engagement platform that enables sales reps to automate and personalize their multi-channel outreach, including email, phone, and social media.

SalesLoft: A sales engagement platform that provides cadence management, email tracking, and conversation intelligence to help sales reps connect with prospects more effectively.

Groove: A sales engagement platform that integrates with CRM systems and provides workflow automation, email templates, and performance analytics.

Sales Intelligence and Prospecting Tools:

ZoomInfo: A B2B database and intelligence platform that provides accurate and comprehensive data on companies and contacts, including firmographic, technographic, and intent data.

LinkedIn Sales Navigator: A social selling tool that helps sales reps find, engage, and build relationships with prospects on LinkedIn.

Clearbit: A data enrichment and prospecting tool that provides real-time company and contact data, including email addresses, phone numbers, and social media profiles.

Sales Enablement and Content Management Platforms:

Seismic: A sales enablement platform that provides content management, personalization, and analytics to help sales reps deliver the right content to the right audience at the right time.

Highspot: A sales enablement platform that offers content management, training, and coaching tools to help sales reps improve their skills and performance.

Showpad: A sales enablement platform that provides content management, presentation tools, and buyer engagement insights to help sales reps deliver more effective sales conversations.

Sales Analytics and Forecasting Tools:

InsightSquared: A sales analytics platform that provides real-time visibility into sales pipeline, performance, and forecasting, and helps sales leaders make data-driven decisions.

Clari: A revenue operations platform that provides AI-powered forecasting, pipeline management, and deal inspection to help sales teams improve accuracy and efficiency.

Aviso: An AI-powered sales forecasting and risk management platform that helps sales teams predict and optimize revenue outcomes.

Sales Coaching and Training Platforms:

Gong: A conversation intelligence platform that analyzes sales calls and provides insights and feedback to help sales reps improve their skills and performance.

Chorus: A conversation intelligence platform that records, transcribes, and analyzes sales calls to help sales teams identify best practices and coaching opportunities.

Brainshark: A sales training and coaching platform that provides online courses, assessments, and reinforcement tools to help sales reps develop and retain their skills.

When selecting sales tech tools, organizations should consider factors such as their sales process, team size, budget, and integration requirements. It is also important to involve sales reps and leaders in the evaluation and selection process to ensure buy-in and adoption. Additionally, organizations should provide adequate training and support to help sales reps leverage the tools effectively and realize their full potential.

Additional Reading and Learning Resources

Continuous learning and development are crucial for sales professionals to stay ahead of the curve and adapt to the ever-changing sales landscape. Here are some additional reading and learning resources to help sales reps and leaders expand their knowledge and skills:

Books:

"Never Split the Difference" by Chris Voss and Tahl Raz: A practical guide on negotiation techniques and strategies, written by a former FBI hostage negotiator.

"The Challenger Sale" by Matthew Dixon and Brent Adamson: A research-based approach to sales that emphasizes the importance of challenging customers' assumptions and providing unique insights.

"Spin Selling" by Neil Rackham: A classic sales book that introduces the SPIN (Situation, Problem, Implication, Need-payoff) selling method for complex B2B sales.

"The Sales Acceleration Formula" by Mark Roberge: A data-driven approach to sales that covers hiring, training, managing, and generating demand.

"Gap Selling" by Keenan: A modern sales methodology that focuses on identifying and solving customers' problems and challenges.

Online Courses and Certifications:

HubSpot Academy: A free online learning platform that offers courses and certifications on inbound sales, sales enablement, and sales management.

Coursera Sales Training: A collection of online courses and specializations on sales, offered by universities and industry experts.

LinkedIn Learning Sales Courses: A library of on-demand courses and videos on sales skills, techniques, and strategies, taught by industry professionals.

RAIN Group Sales Training: A sales training company that provides online and in-person courses on consultative selling, negotiation, and sales leadership.

SalesBuzz Sales Training: An online sales training platform

that offers courses and certifications on prospecting, objection handling, closing, and more.

Blogs and Websites:

Sales Hacker: A community-driven blog and resource hub that covers the latest trends, best practices, and tools in sales.

HubSpot Sales Blog: A blog that provides insights, tips, and strategies on inbound sales, sales enablement, and sales technology.

LinkedIn Sales Blog: A blog that shares thought leadership and best practices on social selling, sales leadership, and customer engagement.

Gong Labs: A research and insights hub that analyzes sales conversations and provides data-driven recommendations for sales excellence.

OpenView Labs: A blog and resource center that covers sales, marketing, and product-led growth strategies for B2B software companies.

Podcasts:

The Sales Hacker Podcast: A weekly podcast that features interviews with sales leaders, experts, and practitioners on the latest trends and strategies in sales.

Make It Happen Mondays: A motivational podcast hosted by John Barrows, a sales trainer and consultant, that shares tips and techniques for sales success.

The Salesman Podcast: A daily podcast that interviews sales professionals, psychologists, and authors on the art and science of sales.

Conversations with Women in Sales: A podcast that highlights the stories and insights of successful women in sales and leadership roles.

The Buyer's Mind: A podcast that explores the psychology and behavior of B2B buyers and provides strategies for sales professionals to influence and persuade them.

By leveraging these reading and learning resources, sales professionals can gain new perspectives, skills, and best practices to improve their performance and advance their careers. It is important to set aside dedicated time for learning and development, and to apply the insights and techniques in real-world sales situations. Additionally, sales leaders should encourage and support their teams' continuous learning and provide opportunities for knowledge sharing and collaboration.

Online Communities and Networks

Online communities and networks have become valuable resources for sales professionals to connect, learn, and grow with their peers and experts in the field. Here are some of the top online communities and networks for sales:

LinkedIn Groups:

Sales Best Practices: A group for sales professionals to share and discuss best practices, strategies, and techniques for success.

B2B Technology Sales Community: A group for technology sales professionals to network, share insights, and stay up-to-date on industry trends.

Women in Sales: A group for women sales professionals to connect, support, and empower each other in their careers.

Facebook Groups:

Sales Talk with Sales Pros: A private group for sales professionals to ask questions, share advice, and discuss sales-related topics.

SaaS Sales Professionals: A group for SaaS sales professionals to network, share best practices, and discuss industry trends and challenges.

RevGenius: A community for revenue leaders and professionals to learn, collaborate, and grow together.

Slack Communities:

Sales Hacker: A Slack community for sales professionals to connect, share insights, and participate in discussions and events.

Thursday Night Sales: A Slack community for B2B sales professionals to network, learn, and support each other.

Modern Sales Pros: A Slack community for sales enablement and operations professionals to share best practices and resources.

Online Forums and Discussion Boards:

SalesGravy: An online forum for sales professionals to ask questions, share advice, and discuss sales-related topics.

Quora Sales: A question-and-answer platform where sales professionals can ask and answer sales-related questions and share their expertise.

Reddit Sales: A subreddit for sales professionals to discuss sales strategies, techniques, and challenges.

Virtual Events and Conferences:

Sales 3.0 Conference: A virtual conference that brings together sales leaders and experts to discuss the latest trends and strategies in sales.

AA-ISP Digital Sales World: A virtual conference that focuses on inside sales and digital sales strategies and best practices.

Outbound Conference: A virtual conference that covers outbound sales strategies, techniques, and tools for B2B sales teams.

By participating in these online communities and networks, sales professionals can:

- Connect with like-minded professionals and expand their network
- Learn from the experiences and best practices of others in the field
- Stay up-to-date on the latest trends, tools, and strategies in sales
- Get advice and support for specific sales challenges and questions
- Share their own insights and expertise and build their personal brand
- Participate in virtual events, webinars, and discussions to enhance their skills and knowledge
- To make the most out of these online communities and networks, sales professionals should:
- Be active and engaged by posting questions, sharing insights, and participating in discussions
- Be respectful and professional in their interactions with others
- Follow the rules and guidelines of each community and network
- Provide value and support to others, not just seek help for themselves
- Connect and follow up with individuals they meet and build meaningful relationships
- Apply the insights and best practices they learn in their own sales activities and share their results and feedback
- By leveraging these online communities and networks, sales professionals can accelerate their learning, expand their network, and ultimately improve their sales performance and career growth.

CONCLUSION AND KEY TAKEAWAYS

Summarizing Core Concepts

Throughout this book, we have explored the key concepts, strategies, and best practices for achieving success in the era of tech-powered sales. Here is a summary of the core concepts covered:

The Evolution of Sales in the Digital Era: Sales has undergone a significant transformation in recent years, driven by advancements in technology and changing customer expectations. Sales professionals must adapt to these changes and leverage technology to stay competitive.

Foundational Sales Skills: While technology has transformed sales, fundamental skills such as adaptability, curiosity, empathy, storytelling, problem-solving, resilience, and collaboration remain critical for success.

Building a Modern Sales Strategy: A effective sales strategy in the tech-powered era involves identifying ideal customer profiles, developing a compelling value narrative, and aligning sales and marketing efforts.

Sales Technology Stack: The sales tech stack includes essential tools for customer relationship management, sales engagement, sales intelligence, sales enablement, forecasting, and analytics. Organizations must carefully select and integrate these tools to optimize their sales processes.

Artificial Intelligence in Sales: AI-powered tools can enhance various aspects of sales, including lead scoring, predictive forecasting, personalized recommendations, sentiment analysis, and conversational AI. Sales teams must learn to effectively leverage AI to improve efficiency and effectiveness.

Sales and Marketing Alignment: Aligning sales and marketing is crucial for creating a unified revenue strategy. This involves establishing shared goals and metrics, integrated planning and execution, shared data and insights, and aligned incentives and rewards.

Optimizing Sales Processes: Streamlining sales processes with technology, implementing sales enablement tools, and adopting data-driven decision making can significantly improve sales performance and efficiency.

Managing and Scaling Sales Teams: Effective sales team management in the tech-driven era involves providing continuous training and development, establishing clear performance metrics and KPIs, and building a resilient sales culture.

Future of Sales: The future of sales will be shaped by advancements in conversational AI, augmented and virtual reality, predictive and prescriptive analytics, sales automation, and blockchain technology. Sales professionals must proactively prepare for these changes.

Ethical Considerations: As sales teams increasingly rely on technology and data, it is crucial to consider the ethical implications and establish guidelines for responsible use, data privacy, and transparency.

By understanding and applying these core concepts, sales professionals and organizations can effectively navigate the tech-powered sales landscape, drive better results, and create value for their customers.

Actionable Insights for Sales Success

To help you translate the knowledge gained from this book into tangible results, here are some actionable insights and recommendations for achieving sales success in the tech-powered era:

Assess your current sales tech stack: Evaluate your existing sales tools and identify gaps or areas for improvement. Consider how well your tools integrate with each other and support your sales processes. Make a plan to optimize your tech stack based on your specific needs and goals.

Invest in sales training and development: Provide your sales team with continuous learning opportunities to develop both technical skills and foundational sales skills. Encourage participation in online courses, workshops, and conferences, and create a culture of knowledge sharing and peer learning.

Leverage data and analytics: Utilize the data generated by your sales tools to gain insights into customer behavior, sales performance, and market trends. Use these insights to make data-driven decisions, optimize your sales strategies, and identify areas for improvement.

Experiment with AI-powered tools: Identify specific areas where AI can enhance your sales processes, such as lead scoring, predictive forecasting, or conversational AI. Start with small pilot projects and measure the impact before scaling up.

Foster sales and marketing alignment: Establish regular communication channels and collaborative processes between sales and marketing teams. Develop shared goals, metrics, and content strategies to ensure a consistent customer experience across the buyer's journey.

Optimize your sales processes: Conduct a thorough analysis of your current sales processes and identify opportunities for automation, streamlining, and improvement. Implement sales enablement tools and best practices to support your team's efficiency and effectiveness.

Focus on customer-centricity: Put the customer at the center of your sales strategies and decisions. Continuously gather and analyze customer feedback, preferences, and behavior data to inform your approach and deliver personalized, value-added experiences.

Build a resilient sales culture: Foster a sales culture that values adaptability, collaboration, continuous learning, and customer focus. Lead by example and provide your team with the support, resources, and recognition they need to thrive in the face of challenges and change.

Stay ahead of future trends: Keep a pulse on the latest advancements in sales technology and customer behavior trends. Attend industry events, join online communities, and read relevant publications to stay informed and proactively prepare for the future of sales.

Prioritize ethics and transparency: Develop clear guidelines and policies for the ethical use of sales technology and data. Ensure that your team understands and adheres to these principles, and communicate transparently with customers about how their data is being used and protected.

By implementing these actionable insights, you can set your sales team up for success in the tech-powered era. Remember that achieving sales excellence is an ongoing journey that requires continuous learning, adaptation, and improvement.

Continuous Learning and Adaptation

The world of sales is constantly evolving, and the pace of change is only accelerating in the tech-powered era. To stay competitive and relevant, sales professionals and organizations must embrace a mindset of continuous learning and adaptation. Here are some strategies for making continuous learning and adaptation a core part of your sales culture:

Cultivate a growth mindset: Encourage your sales team to view challenges and setbacks as opportunities for learning and growth, rather than failures. Lead by example and demonstrate a willingness to learn from mistakes and try new approaches.

Make learning a priority: Allocate time and resources for your sales team to engage in learning activities, such as attending workshops, completing online courses, or reading industry publications. Set learning goals and track progress as part of your team's performance metrics.

Foster a culture of experimentation: Empower your sales team to test new ideas, techniques, and technologies in a safe and supportive environment. Celebrate both successes and failures as valuable learning experiences, and encourage sharing of best practices and lessons learned.

Leverage technology for learning: Utilize the vast array of online learning resources and tools available, such as webinars, podcasts, and virtual reality simulations, to provide your team with flexible and engaging learning experiences.

Encourage peer learning: Create opportunities for your sales team to learn from each other, such as through mentoring programs, peer coaching, or regular knowledge-sharing sessions. Encourage collaboration and cross-functional learning to break down silos and promote innovation.

Seek external perspectives: Attend industry conferences, join professional networks, and engage with customers and partners to gain diverse perspectives and insights. Encourage your team to bring back new ideas and best practices to share with the rest of the organization.

Regularly assess and adapt: Continuously assess your sales strategies, processes, and tools to identify areas for improvement and adaptation. Use data and feedback to inform your decisions and pivot quickly when needed.

Celebrate learning and growth: Recognize and reward individuals and teams who demonstrate a commitment to continuous learning and improvement. Celebrate milestones and successes, and share stories of learning and adaptation to inspire others.

By embedding continuous learning and adaptation into your sales culture, you can build a team that is resilient, agile, and equipped to thrive in the face of change and uncertainty. Remember that learning is not a one-time event, but a lifelong journey that requires curiosity, humility, and a willingness to embrace new ideas and possibilities.

In conclusion, the era of tech-powered sales presents both challenges and opportunities for sales professionals and organizations. By leveraging the right technologies, strategies, and skills, you can unlock new levels of efficiency, effectiveness, and customer value. However, success in this era requires more than just adopting the latest tools and techniques. It requires a fundamental shift in mindset and culture towards continuous learning, adaptation, and customer-centricity.

Throughout this book, we have explored the key concepts, best practices, and actionable insights for achieving sales success in the tech-powered era. From building a modern sales strategy and optimizing your sales processes, to leveraging AI and aligning with marketing, we have covered a wide range of topics to help you stay ahead of the curve.

But the learning and growth do not stop here. The world of sales will continue to evolve, and new technologies, trends, and customer expectations will emerge. To stay competitive and relevant, you must make continuous learning and adaptation a core part of your sales culture and daily practice.

So, take the insights and strategies you have gained from this book and put them into action. Experiment, iterate, and learn from your successes and failures. Stay curious, humble, and open to new possibilities. And most importantly, never lose sight of the human element at the heart of sales – the relationships, trust, and value you build with your customers.

By embracing the tech-powered era with a growth mindset and customer-centric approach, you can not only survive but thrive in the future of sales. You can become a sales leader who not only adapts to change but harnesses it to drive meaningful impact and success for your team, your organization, and your customers.

Disclaimer:

The information contained in this book is provided for educational and informational purposes only and is not intended as a substitute for professional advice. The author and publisher disclaim all responsibility for any errors or omissions in the information provided and for any consequences arising from the use of the information contained herein.

While every effort has been made to ensure the accuracy and completeness of the information presented, the author and publisher cannot guarantee that the information is up-to-date or error-free. The author and publisher shall not be held liable for any damages arising from the use of the information contained in this book.

The views and opinions expressed in this book are those of the author and do not necessarily reflect the views or opinions of the publisher. The author and publisher do not endorse or recommend any specific products, services, or treatments mentioned in this book.

The reader is advised to consult with a qualified professional before making any decisions or taking any action based on the information contained in this book.

Other works by Kim Domingo Reyes

https://hi.switchy.io/kimdomingoreyes

www.ingramcontent.com/pod-product-compliance
Lightning Source LLC
Chambersburg PA
CBHW050100230526
45470CB00004B/1612